A Theatrical Feast in
New York

A THEATRICAL FEAST IN
NEW YORK

ELIZABETH SHARLAND

FOREWORD BY ROSEMARY HARRIS

SUTTON PUBLISHING

First published in the United Kingdom in 2004 by
Sutton Publishing Limited · Phoenix Mill
Thrupp · Stroud · Gloucestershire · GL5 2BU

Copyright © Elizabeth Sharland, 2004

British Library Cataloguing in Publication Data
A catalogue record for this book is available from the British
Library.

ISBN 0-7509-3719-X

Typeset in 11.5/15pt Melior.
Typesetting and origination by
Sutton Publishing Limited.
Printed and bound in England by
J.H. Haynes & Co. Ltd, Sparkford.

DEDICATED TO
Max Klimavicius
Sean Ricketts
Ivan Lesica

Contents

Foreword by Rosemary Harris   ix

Acknowledgments   xi

Introduction   1

1   Famous Theatrical Restaurants   6

2   Hotels for the Stars   24

3   The Players Club   36

4   The Lambs Club   44

5   The Friars Club   51

6   Early British Stars of Broadway   62

7   Dorothy Parker and the Algonquin Round Table   71

8   Restaurant Row and the Fringe Theaters of New York   93

9   Ivor Novello's Favorites   100

10   Following in Noël Coward's Footsteps   111

11   Legendary Figures of the Theater   127

12   Theatrical Nibbles and Nuggets   143

13   Critics' Flavors   152

14   Modern Stars . . . or Sugar and Spice   164

15   Three Walks through New York's Theaterland   186

Epilogue: Food for the Spirit   198

Bibliography   202

Index   204

Foreword

On my first arrival in New York on board the *Queen Mary* in 1952 I spent the night at the Algonquin Hotel, before the producers moved me to more modest accommodation! That evening I witnessed Broadway dimming its lights in tribute to Gertrude Lawrence. I was taken to Sardi's for dinner, sat with Moss Hart, his wife Kitty, his brother Bernie and their friends at his big round table in the middle of the restaurant, and was introduced to steak tartare. All the Broadway producers had their own tables in those days. Producers usually eat dinner before the show whereas actors prefer to wait till after the performance. I watched fascinated as the waiter mixed the raw egg and raw meat together with a few chopped onions at the table. As Shakespeare said, "See the players well bestowed." Steak Diane was popular then too as well as prawn cocktails, and when we couldn't afford to go to Sardi's we'd go to Downey's on Eighth Avenue where the photos on the wall were of aspiring actors instead of the celebrated caricatures in Sardi's.

In 1956 George Grizzard and I, when we were on Broadway in *The Disenchanted*, used to go on matinée days between the shows to Sardi's, have a martini and a steak, then return to our dressing rooms and sleep on our cots like babies.

Today it is rare to see a waiter cooking a dish beside your table. Perhaps it is because patrons might sue if their hair or clothing catches fire. It is a custom that seemed to be part of that era of the golden age of Broadway. Fortunately Elizabeth has rediscovered some of the memories these places hold in the world of the theater which is Broadway.

Rosemary Harris

Acknowledgments

Let me thank all the people for the help and advice they have given me for this book, as well as the permission to use material and brief excerpts from their lives and works. The following list includes many now sadly no longer with us, and I would like to thank their estates for permission to quote from books and articles.

Eileen Atkins, Clive Barnes, Brendan Behan, Michael Billington, Gyles Brandreth, Dennis Brown, Jared Brown, Quentin Crisp, Barry Day, James R. Gaines, Patrick Garland, Lewis Hardee, Rosemary Harris, Kitty Carlisle Hart, André Jammet, H. Peter Kriendler, John Lahr, George Lang, Marion Mead, John Miller, Sheridan Morley, Dorothy Parker, Dan Poole, Vincent Sardi Jr., Ned Sherrin, Robert Treboux, Paul Webb, James Villas, Billie Whitelaw, P.G. Wodehouse.

Every effort has been made to trace all copyright holders, but if any have inadvertently been overlooked, the author will be pleased to make the necessary arrangements at the first opportunity.

Introduction

If there's anywhere in America that deserves the phrase "melting pot," then it's New York. The gateway to America yet in many ways separate from it, New York reflects its position as both the entry to the New World and the strongest link to the Old.

Theater as we know it began in Europe, and New York, founded by the Dutch but rapidly conquered by the British, shows its English heritage not just in its language but through its theater.

This book explores that connection, looking at the New York theater scene, and at how food—New York's other strong point, along with Art Deco skyscrapers, yellow cabs, and art galleries—has literally and figuratively sustained the theater industry and its greatest stars.

Given New York's Atlantic setting this book will look at British as well as well as American stars: at where they ate, lived and loved, and at how so much of what makes Broadway tick takes place as much in a restaurant as in a rehearsal room.

Private dinner parties, too, along with Noël Coward's trays of "something eggy" in grand hotel suites, and the private house that inspired one of his greatest comedies, *Hay Fever*, can also be found in this record of the glamor and the gourmets that have made the Great White Way arguably the most exciting street in the world.

Among the places we visit in this book are the Algonquin Hotel, where the ghosts of Dorothy Parker and her Round Table circle can still be sensed, passing acerbic yet irresistibly funny comments on the modern-day guests. We pass through the doors of Sardi's to enjoy the picture-lined room, every one of whose caricatures represents someone famous who has dined at this most theatrical of Manhattan restaurants.

No account of New York would be complete without reference to its most famous hotel, the Plaza, located on the edge of Central Park, where generations of aspiring actors have survived on sandwiches and thermos flasks of hot, strong coffee, dreaming of the day they find their place in the sun and their seat at a table . . .

We also explore the Waldorf Astoria, where theater stars were matched by such members of the international jet set as the ex-King Edward VIII of England and his American wife.

Wallis Simpson, far from being the parvenu the British press often made her out to be, was in fact a member of the American aristocracy (albeit a poor relation until she found her real-life prince) and the Americans have gentlemen's (and ladies') clubs every bit as grand and as interesting as their British equivalents in St. James's, London.

The first of the theatrical clubs that we focus on is the Players, the New York equivalent of the Garrick Club, and which Sir John Gielgud—who was as popular in the States, where he played a memorable Hamlet in the 1930s and toured his one-man show, *The Ages of Man*, in the 1950s, as he was in Britain—called his "second home."

Next we look at the Lambs Club, named after the English essayist and theater critic Charles Lamb, then move on to the Friars, whose famous "roasts" are still givon for membeis uf Lhe theatrical profession. In the past you could rub shoulders with Michael Todd and Elizabeth Taylor, whereas today you might see Jeremy Irons or Natasha Richardson.

We go back to the nineteenth century to learn about the theatrical and culinary triumphs of luminaries like Charles Dickens, Oscar Wilde, and Lillie Langtry, then move forward to the early twentieth century, where we celebrate the New York connections of giants like Noël Coward and Ivor Novello, following especially in Sir Noël's footsteps as on successive visits to New York he moved from being a young and at times literally starving would-be star to a real-life one with theatrical New York at his feet.

Other legendary Broadway names who dined and dated in this most cosmopolitan of cities include P.G. Wodehouse (best known as a comic author but a prolific writer of lyrics and co-author of the book of Cole Porter's 1934 masterpiece

Anything Goes) and the critics Kenneth Tynan (from Britain) and Frank Rich from the States.

Modern-day stars we follow from stage door to dinner include Judi Dench, Maggie Smith, the Redgraves—Vanessa, Lynn, and Corin—Julie Andrews, Angela Lansbury, Sir Peter Hall, Sir David Hare, Sir Cameron Mackintosh, and Lord Lloyd Webber.

We round the book off with three walks that take you through New York, leading you to or past many of the places described earlier, so you can literally follow in the footsteps of the stars, directors, agents, and critics described in these pages.

Whether discussing theatrical giants of the past like Alfred Lunt and Lynne Fontanne, Moss Hart and George F. Kaufman, or more recent stars like Carol Channing and Yul Brynner, this book provides its own equivalent of the handprints that are Hollywood's way of immortalizing its stars. This being the theater and New York—the city which boasts the greatest variety of cuisine within the most compact space, in the whole world—the impressions the stars have left are not in cement but written in the memories and imaginations of anyone who has ever enjoyed a night at a Broadway theater.

In an age when going to a restaurant is almost as much a part of a theatrical night out as going to the theater itself—hence the success of Yasmina Reza's very short play *Art*, and a succession of other brief and stylish plays that left plenty of time to discuss them over a relaxed dinner at Sardi's—we celebrate not only past pleasures of table and theater, but current and future ones, looking in particular at the newly-developed Theater Row.

We haven't written about any night clubs in this book as places like El Morocco and the Stork Club closed years ago and need a book of their own.

New York is always in a state of renewal—that's one of its greatest strengths—and this book celebrates both the continuity and the change of its theater district, theater followers, and stars. If you are already at life's top table this is a book where you will recognize your favorite haunts and fellow thespians; if you are on your way there this will be a guide and an appetizer as you head, star-struck, towards the banquet that is Broadway.

1

Famous Theatrical Restaurants

It is almost *de rigueur* to start a visit to the theater
with an early dinner or at least drinks at a famous
restaurant in theaterland. Some restaurants have
little flags on the tables for people going on to a
show, to indicate this to the waiter. Sardi's restaurant is packed to the caricatures on the walls at
7 p.m., but by curtain time at 8 p.m. it is deserted.
All around the streets from 42nd to 50th is the
jostling, excitement, and anticipation of theater-
goers in their hundreds. No other section of a city
is so focused on theater as Broadway between 7:30
and 8 p.m. on any night.

At the turn of the last century there were
Churchill's, Maxim's, Delmonico's, Luchow's,
the Everglades, Pabst's, Shanley's Moulin Rouge,
and before that Rector's. Broadway's nightlife
would shortly be replaced by speakeasies and
gangland murders.

Rector's was the place to be seen. With huge
mirrors on the walls, gilt and velvet everywhere,
the décor was Louis XV; there were one hundred
tables downstairs and seventy-five upstairs. Actors
Edwin Booth, Fanny Kemble, and Dion Boucicault

were playing in the theaters. One of the most popular producers then was Charles Frohman, who preferred British plays and brought them over from England.

Rector's was between 43rd and 44th Street in Times Square. He said, "I found Broadway a quiet little lane of ham and eggs in 1889, and left it a full-blown avenue of lobsters and champagne." No play was a hit unless it was followed by a reception at Rector's. Sarah Bernhardt, Ellen Terry, Henry Irving, Lillie Langtry, and Herbert Beerbohm Tree were seen there, Tree even when he had received a bad review from John Palmer of his Shylock; "Go and see Shylock as Mr. Tree."

The British stars rubbed shoulders at Rector's with Victor Herbert, Henry Miller, and Theodore Dreiser. There is a story that George M. Cohan tried to save Rector's from closing but failed. Nowadays the most celebrated theater restaurant with an incredible theater history comparable to Rector's is just around the corner from where Rector's used to be—**Sardi's** at 234 West 44th Street. It is legendary in the theater world. A family business handed down from father to son, Sardi senior opened the restaurant in its current location in 1927. The caricatures on the walls show the best-known actors, actresses, playwrights, and directors. Walter Winchell was one of Broadway's most powerful columnists from 1928 to 1960. He loved Sardi's, and he used to write about it in his column which was nationally syndicated, so millions of people linked Sardi's with the celebrated stars.

In Vincent Sardi's book *Off the Wall at Sardi's* he tells many stories about the actors who have dined there, and also how the caricatures are precious mementos to him. Often the stars refuse to sign their pictures, but Sardi hangs them up anyway. Because the collection is always being added to, many of the older ones are "retired." They are now in the Library of the Performing Arts at the Lincoln Center.

When asked who was the most impressive person he had ever met in Sardi's, Vincent said that some of them weren't in the theater at all: President Harry Truman, Eleanor Roosevelt, and an all-time favorite Ernie Kovacs. He says, "I don't mind not being a doctor, I'm taking care of people, but in a different way."

Vincent Sardi Jr. offered credit to actors years ago, feeding them when they were fresh out of money. José Ferrer said that Vincent was partly responsible for his winning his Oscar for *Cyrano*. "By feeding me while I was financing *Cyrano* on the stage, he made it possible for me to get a movie offer and eventually to play the part on film. I ran up a bill for $1,700, but Vincent never mentioned the bill."

Sardi's is the place where the first night parties are held. Tradition has it that the reason is because the *New York Times* is just next door, and the papers get delivered here as soon as they are printed. Careers are made and broken by the next review. The cast stay up waiting for the papers and wait for the first light of dawn. As Sardi himself said, "You can always tell how the box-office is going to behave the next day by what happens in Sardi's after the reviews come out. If they're good, we start to hear 'Captain, a bottle of champagne and the food menu.' If the reviews aren't good, all we hear is 'Check, please.'"

In his youth, Vincent played three walk-on parts on Broadway, and appeared in two television plays, in both of which he played himself with Sardi's as the setting. He still appears in the restaurant from time to time, but since a recent heart operation he spends much of his time at home in Vermont. Sardi's is where Laurence Olivier, after his show on Broadway, dined with Noël Coward to tell him his marriage to Vivien Leigh was over. They were the "Royal Pair" at that stage. Both in London and New York they were household names.

Sardi also goes on to say that P.R. and press agents always want their stars to sit in the front of the restaurant, but he maintains that if they cross the room to a back table, everyone in the restaurant will see them. This does not apply at a smaller restaurant up by the Lincoln Center. The **Café des Artistes**, at 1 West 67th Street, is on the ground floor of an apartment building called the Hotel des Artistes, which was home at various times to Noël Coward, Edna Ferber, Isadora Duncan, and Rudolf Valentino. It is probably best known for the murals, painted in the 1930s by Howard Chandler Christy, who was initially a celebrated magazine illustrator, then a fashionable portrait painter. The murals depict pretty, nude wood-nymphs, dancing around and generally disporting themselves. The names of the paintings are: *The Parrot Girl*, *The Swing Girl*, *Ponce de Leon*, *Fall*, *Spring*, and *The Fountain Girl*. In 1917, Christy was one of the earliest residents in the newly-built Hotel des Artistes—which is not a hotel, but a residential building along the lines of Parisian mansions. It originally housed a private ballroom, a swimming pool, and a squash court, and, of course, the famous restaurant on the ground floor.

Christy's latter profession as a society and government officials' portrait painter put him in the limelight wherever he went: newspapers published interviews detailing his latest portraits, the clothes he and Mrs. Christy wore, and who they were with. This time, his lifestyle, not that of the people he depicted in his earlier illustrations, was what the public admired.

The Café was a meeting place between creative efforts, offering reasonably priced food flavored with good conversation; and it also served an essential function for residents of the Hotel des Artistes. Because the sumptuous duplexes had only tiny pullman kitchens, the famed tenants bought their own raw ingredients, sent them down to the kitchen of the Café des Artistes with instructions for cooking, and the kitchen then sent dinners upstairs on dumbwaiters precisely at the time requested. To keep cold foods in the pantries of the apartments, a Rube Goldberg-like 20-ton ice machine in the basement circulated ice-water into each apartment's icebox.

In an era long past, Fannie Hurst, Marcel Duchamp, Maurice Maeterlinck, Isadora Duncan, Alexander Woollcott, and Mayor Fiorello La Guardia had their regular tables at the Café. It is now a meeting-place for some of the most famous names in the artistic and entertainment worlds. Isaac Stern, Kathleen Turner, James Levine, Itzhak Perlman, and Paul Newman are among the regulars. The ambience is exceptional, perhaps the most romantic in New York, taking its tone from the carefree young nymphs frolicking in the murals and the flowers, plants, and chandeliers in the main dining-room.

George Lang, the owner, is an exceptional man who runs two other large restaurants in his home town of Budapest. His best-selling autobiography *Nobody Knows the Truffles I've Seen* tells the story of his extraordinary life. Born in Hungary, he was destined for the concert stage, but his world suddenly collapsed when at nineteen he was incarcerated in a forced labor camp, never to see his parents again. His planned escape from Hungary in a hired hearse backfired, and he was forced to walk through minefields to reach the Austrian border. He arrived in New York in 1946 and started work at the Four Seasons. His book has a lively cast of characters, ranging from Pavarotti and James Beard to President Clinton and Pope John Paul II. His office is next door to the Café and he is often seen in the restaurant with the stars of opera, Hollywood, and Broadway. In the past he held orchestrated banquets at the Waldorf for Kruschev, Queen Elizabeth, and Princess Grace, and is well known throughout Manhattan by all the top chefs, food editors, and celebrities.

Prohibition, or more formally the "Eighteenth Amendment to the Constitution of the United States of America," became law on January 17, 1920. It had a variety of effects, but perhaps one of the happiest was the institution of one of the best restaurants in New York, **21**, at number 21 West 52nd Street.

It started in 1922 as a speakeasy called the Red Head located in the Village, moved to Washington Place, changing its name in the process to the Fronton. Early patrons of the Fronton were Edna St. Vincent Millay, Herbert Swope of the *New York World*, and James J. Walker, mayor of New York. The proprietors were Jack Kriendler and Charlie Berns, and bit by bit the speakeasy became also a restaurant with a professional chef and a wine list. Because of subway construction and the resultant dislocation, the Fronton moved first to 42 West 49th Street, changing the name again to the Puncheon. Prices were deliberately kept high and customers were discreetly but carefully vetted.

The restaurant attracted patrons such as John O'Hara (author of *Butterfield 8*), Robert Benchley, as well as, briefly, Dorothy Parker, playwright George Kaufman, Alexander Woollcott, Edna Ferber, H.L. Mencken, Frank Crowninshield (editor of *Vanity Fair*), Scott Fitzgerald, and other writers and reporters. The owners had good connections with the press and the city police, but the Federal police who were responsible for enforcing Prohibition raided the Puncheon several times. When the lease ran out, Jack and Charlie were determined to own their next location, so they bought the house at 21 West 52nd Street in 1928, intending to move their speakeasy-cum-restaurant there in 1930.

However, the Great Stock Market Crash started in October 1929; two months later Jack and Charlie moved to 21 after a huge rowdy party at the Puncheon, in the course of which the wrought-iron gate of the 49th Street restaurant was removed and next day installed in front of 21.

By this time Jack and Charlie had made a good deal of money, and to assure the patronage of their regulars, many of whom had been severely hurt financially by the Wall Street Crash, they extended credit, held onto worthless cheques until they were good, and made long-term loans.

Prohibition was still a problem, and the owners of 21 spent a fortune converting the restaurant into a place immune from raids, after a raid instigated by Walter Winchell, who, infuriated by being denied admission to 21, published a newspaper item under the headline "A Place Never Raided, Jack & Charlie's at 21 West Fifty-second Street." This of course ensured that 21 was quickly raided; Jack and Charlie were arrested. The subsequent press publicity was an embarrassment to the U.S. Treasury Department, the search warrant that the Feds had used was invalidated, Jack and Charlie were simply fined 50 dollars each for possession of liquor, and returned to business as usual.

A final raid in 1932 was reported in the *New York Times*: "Wet spot goes dry as raiders arrive. Agents Get a Cordial Welcome but No Liquor."

Franklin Delano Roosevelt had pledged in his election campaign in 1932 that he would end Prohibition, and upon his election as President another amendment to the Constitution to abolish Prohibition was adopted by the two houses of Congress and ratified by the states in December 1933.

The abolition of Prohibition naturally reduced some of the strain of running the perfect speakeasy, which at a stroke of the pen became a legal enterprise, but seriously increased the competition. Profits began to fall; in this dilemma Jack and Charlie got the brilliant idea of creating and possessing a monopoly on Ballantine's Scotch which they had already made the standard scotch at 21. They were able to persuade the distiller to grant them this, but on account of a Federal ban on wholesalers being also in the retail liquor business,

Jack and Charlie dissolved their partnership on paper; Jack being responsible for the retail end, Charlie taking on "21 Brands," the wholesaler of Ballantine's. Other wines and spirits were later added to the merchandise, and subsequently specialty foods.

David Niven, the actor, was briefly employed by them as a liquor salesman. A photograph of Niven labelled "OUR FIRST AND WORST SALESMAN" was hung up in the bar of 21.

Eventually business at 21 recovered, to the extent that more space was needed. Jack and Charlie already owned the house next door, number 19, and the two buildings were amalgamated by breaking down the wall between, an event which was celebrated by another rowdy party in 1936.

The story of 21 revolves around good food (but not always gourmet food), great wine, celebrity, status, and above all, high prices and money. However, its habitués come back over and over again to the atmosphere generated within, one of friendliness, good humor, comfort, and elegance. In every decade it has been a magnet for celebrities of every kind, some with genius or talent, some by their wealth and/or social position, but the expectation has been that all the patrons are people that one would be delighted to have as guests in one's own home, people who are polite and well-bred, and invariably well-behaved (not always the case, but one can't have everything).

You'll see a plaque at the bar that reads "Bogie's Corner" because Humphrey Bogart was such a regular, sipping gin fizzes while trailing cigarette smoke across the room.

La Caravelle at 33 West 54th Street was known not only for its exquisite French cuisine but for the beautifully illuminated colorful murals of Parisian scenes painted by Jean Pagis, who was a student of Dufy, and for the elegant ambience of a luxury restaurant, with fresh roses on each table.

Le Pavillon ceased to be fashionable when Henri Soule died in 1966, and the Colony fell out of favor soon after that and had to close, as did Le Voisin. Many of the fashionable clientèle moved to La Caravelle. It became the favorite luncheon rendezvous of Grace Kelly and Jackie Kennedy (all the Kennedys liked it), and still caters to stars of the stage and screen, writers, producers, and successful businessmen. Recently Michael Douglas celebrated his birthday there with his wife Catherine Zeta-Jones. David Brown, the celebrated film producer, lunched there regularly.

The owner and general manager, André Jammet, has a fascinating family history. His grandfather built and ran the Hotel Bristol in Paris, and he and his brother opened a restaurant in Dublin called Jammet's which, during the 1950s and '60s, was the most celebrated restaurant in Dublin. Jammet was at La Caravelle for nineteen years, and the barman behind the tiny bar in the room that used to be a speakeasy was there for forty years and has many stories to tell. Concert pianist Vladimir Horowitz used to order his favorite dish (not on the menu) called Poularde Pochée, which was chicken, rice, and vegetables with a very strong chicken stock. Alas, this delightful restaurant closed on May 22, 2004.

From the **Rainbow Room**, which is on the 65th floor of the Rockefeller Center, there is a spectacular view of Manhattan and it is even more breathtaking at night, when the lights of the city are on. It is one of the most romantic dining rooms in New York. The divided staircase descending from behind the orchestra is reminiscent of the Café Royal in London. One can well imagine a dramatic entrance of Marlene Dietrich or Noël Coward descending slowly down on to the bandstand. There is a revolving dance floor, with dancing usually to a large orchestra. Art Deco design continues into the nightclub, Rainbow in the Stars, just along the corridor. It's a night of Gershwin, Cole Porter, and Jerome Kern up in the sky with a New York skyline.

During the great Depression, the construction of the Rockefeller Center gave work to millions. It also gave New York society a new place to drink, dine, and to watch the lights of New York, the Rainbow Room. The Rockefellers opened the Rainbow Room on October 3, 1934, with a gala opening dinner, attended by the cream of New York society, including themselves, the Astors, the Harrimans, and other notables, as well as a crowd of not-so-notable commoners who paid $15 each for the privilege. The French chanteuse Lucienne Boyer sang "Parlez-moi d'Amour," then danced across the revolving dance floor. The management had taken care to avoid the appearance of a commonplace night club. Mlle. Boyer was the first in a long series of French chanteuses at the Rainbow Room, giving two performances a night. She was enormously popular, a pop star in modern terms, written up in magazines which described in detail her wardrobe, her accessories, and the possessions she had brought with her to New York.

The Rainbow Room paid some of its artists, including Bea Lillie, $2,500 a week during the Depression, and hired the best-known bandleaders of the day. Duke Ellington, Peter Duchin, and Louis Armstrong performed there.

In 1962 the Rainbow Room was completely overhauled and returned to its 1930s' condition. The great double staircase was restored, and otherwise the room has been renovated to look exactly as it did before World War II. Nowhere else in New York can one recapture the essence of the 1930s as faithfully as at the Rainbow Room, and for this reason it should be included in any visit to the city.

Like every major restaurant, reservations are essential. Robert Benchley said it first: "If you can get a reservation at the place, it can't be any good." But it is. The Rainbow Room continues to attract an enormous following, not only because of live dance bands and the revolving dance floor, but also its dazzling cocktails and Baked Alaskas, along with the latest in contemporary cuisine, composed of fresh New York State produce.

Elaine's at 1703 Second Avenue (between East 88th and 89th Streets) is the haunt of theater, literary, and film stars. Mary Quant and Jean Muir also made it popular with British dress designers years ago. Woody Allen is a regular. Michael Caine, Clint Eastwood, and writers such as the late George Plimpton are also habitués. Elaine presides over the front tables, and be careful not to be seated in Siberia (the back tables). Elaine herself is a much loved restauranteur who is a patron of the arts.

Le Veau D'Or is a French restaurant at 129 East 60th Street, owned by the born raconteur Robert Treboux, and is still a colorful venue for Francophiles, although its fame was at its highest during the 1970s, when Jackie Kennedy, Grace Kelly, and New York socialites all met here for lunch. Robert is still behind the bar to greet you. James Villas, the former Food and Wine Editor of *Town and Country* magazine for twenty years, writes that this restaurant has virtually been his second home for over forty years. He first dined there as a teenager with his parents, and on the small red banquettes he has negotiated career changes and fallen in and out of love. He has shared "les cuisses de grenouilles" and "la poularde en cocotte" with Craig Claiborne, Elaine Stritch, and Bobby Short, signed book contracts, and watched Tennessee Williams pass out from too much chablis.

Chez Josephine at 414 West 42nd Street is a delightful theatrical bistro and is ideally located in the heart of the theater district. A pioneer in the revival of 42nd Street since 1986, Chez Josephine is a bubbly return to the joie-de-vivre of the 1930s— le Jazz Hot with soul. A tribute to Josephine Baker, the restaurant and its live music exude panache. Recently remodeled, now with a private party room, this landmark jewel is even more romantic with its blue-tin ceiling, red velvet walls, and cavalcade of chandeliers which light up the vintage flavors.

Gallagher's Steak House at 228 West 52nd Street is a well-known steak house with the raw meat displayed in the front window, and it is right in the middle of theaterland. It was first a speakeasy—a Runyonesque gathering place for gamblers, sports personalities, showbiz folk, and other stars of the Broadway firmament. Helen Gallagher and Jack Solomon launched Gallagher's in November 1927, a few nights before the opening of *Funny Face* next door at the Alvin Theater, which is now called the Neil Simon Theater, a brand-new musical by George and Ira Gershwin that starred Fred Astaire and his sister Adele. That changed in 1933, the watershed year that saw the Depression bottom out as FDR took office and delivered on his promise to end Prohibition.

With the sale of liquor now legalized, Helen Gallagher and Jack Solomon brought an entirely new dimension to American cuisine: the nation's first steak house. Today, in its 68th year—58 of them as a steak house—the décor remains exactly as it was and so does the incredible mix of its clientèle: showbiz people from both Coasts; jocks from every calling of the sports world; business types from London, Cairo, Rio de Janeiro, Tokyo, Peoria and, of course, New York; and Big Apple visitors from Connecticut to Cannes. Among them it is not unusual to see such disparate celebrities as Vanessa Redgrave, Jackie Mason, Liz Smith, Oliver North, and Madonna dining all at once within the spacious walls of Gallagher's, unnoticed by one another.

Plain plank floors, wood-panelled walls, and red checked tablecloths give it an informal blending of speakeasy and country inn. The dark walls are covered with photos of Broadway and Hollywood stars, business luminaries, and athletes past and present.

Another very popular restaurant, particularly with the British, is **Langan's** at 150 West 42nd Street. There is a long bar on the right-hand side as you enter the restaurant which has the ambience of an Irish bar where the clientèle are either watching a baseball game on the TV behind the bar or engaged in animated conversation with glasses of Guinness in their hands.

Surprisingly, at the back of the room is the elegant dining area. Photographs of famous past and present stage and screen stars and framed theater posters line the walls. Show tunes play softly in the background, adding to the cheerful theatrical feel of the place. The cuisine is contemporary American, and it serves one of the best three-course pre-theater dinners in the heart of theaterland. It is a favorite spot for actors after the show who come in either for a quick drink or dinner.

Tea & Sympathy at 108 Greenwich Avenue at Seventh Avenue is an authentic amalgamation of English teashop, Mum's kitchen, and workingman's café, right in the heart of New York City. Its success over the last decade has disproven the common American notion that British cuisine is a myth. In fact, tourists from the world over make their way to the unofficial British embassy on Greenwich Avenue to tuck into Welsh rarebit, shepherd's pie, sticky toffee pudding, and the like. Their subsequent delight is evident in the smiles on their faces and the word of mouth that has kept this exquisitely tiny restaurant afloat through thick and thin.

Still, Tea & Sympathy would not be here now were it not for its loyal regulars from the early days. British expats and Anglophile New Yorkers adopted the little teashop before word about the menu got out. Anita Naughton, one of the original waitresses, introduces us to many of these characters in her memoir of the life of the restaurant. Between the drama of the patrons, the kitchen staff, the waitresses, and Nicky, the enigmatic owner, you can see why so many have made Tea & Sympathy a second home. Comfort food and tough love are served up in equal portions.

Together, Anita's depiction of the daily goings-on and Nicky's recipes for her most famous dishes convey the unique charm of the place. One thing you learn from this kitchen confidential is that there is never a bad day to eat at Tea & Sympathy—everything is always delicious! Rupert Everett, Joanna Lumley, Naomi Campbell, Tina Brown, and Harold Evans, part of the regular clientèle, would say so.

2

Hotels for the Stars

When British actors played on Broadway, they generally stayed in hotels. In London, this wasn't so common, although theater people such as Charlie Chaplin, Orson Welles, Somerset Maugham, Noël Coward, and Tallulah Bankhead stayed at the Savoy and the Ritz.

Most of these hotels are in the theater district or within easy reach, the exception being the Waldorf Astoria which is over on the East Side. Probably the best-known one for British actors is the **Algonquin Hotel** on West 44th Street. It has been home to most of the British contingent of actors for over fifty years. What hotel in the world could boast a guest-list like the Algonquin? Noël Coward, Gertrude Lawrence, John Gielgud, Laurence Olivier, Charles Laughton, Bea Lillie, Jonathan Miller, Ian McKellen, Peter Ustinov, David Hare, the Redgraves, Jeremy Irons, Anthony Hopkins, Trevor Nunn, Tom Stoppard, Peter Hall, Angela Lansbury, and Diana Rigg. A few Irish visitors like Lady Gregory and Brendan Behan join distinguished Americans such as Orson Welles, the Barrymores, Douglas Fairbanks (who sold soap to the management before achieving stardom and who spent a honeymoon here), Alfred Lunt, Lillian Gish, Burgess Meredith, Helen Menken, Ina Claire, John Drew, Orson Welles (who also spent a honeymoon here), Ruth Gordon, Dorothy Stickney, and Arthur Hunnicut (who was an Algonquin dishwasher before gaining fame on Broadway and in Hollywood). Walter Huston got up one night in the Oak Room nightclub and sang "September Song," his show-stopper from *Knickbocker Holiday*. Recent visitors include Lily Tomlin, Gordon Davidson, Richard Dreyfuss, Jason Robards, Carroll O'Connor, Tommy Tune, Celeste Holm, Natasha Richardson, Bernadette Peters, Liza Minnelli, and Kevin Kline.

Playwrights, no less than musicians and actors, found a home here. George S. Kaufman (*The Man Who Came to Dinner*) and Edna Ferber (*Dinner at Eight* and her novel *Show Boat*) are perhaps the best known. Lerner and Loewe wrote *My Fair Lady* and *Brigadoon* in Loewe's suite at the Algonquin.

The famous Round Table or, as they called themselves, "The Vicious Circle," consisted of nine regulars of whom the most remembered are Dorothy Parker, George Kaufman, Alexander Woollcott, George Jean Nathan, Robert E. Sherwood (*The Petrified Forest*), Robert Benchley, and Edna Ferber. The group started in 1919 with a lunch given to welcome Alexander Woolcott back to New York and the *New York Times*, on which he was the hated and feared drama critic. After the lunch someone said, "Why don't we do this every day?" And so they did, for ten years.

The Algonquin has played a major role in the history of Broadway and continues to do so today. For years, they have hosted *Playbill*'s monthly George Spelvin lunches, which feature the casts of current Broadway shows. Theater awards voting sessions are held annually behind closed doors. The Algonquin has hosted countless Broadway opening and closing nights. One of the great "closing night" parties was the one in 1933 that marked the end of Prohibition, with Marilyn Miller and Clifton Webb, stars of *As Thousands Cheer*, leading the revelers that thronged the Algonquin's lobby.

Near the conclusion of his 1977 book about the Round Table, *Wit's End*, James R. Gaines writes, "None of them ever bid a genuine good-by to the Round Table—one, that is to say, which neither excoriated it for its foolishness nor pretended that the group had been fabricated by the press for its own delight, the line to which Kaufman resorted in later years. Perhaps, as they avoided with humor the vulnerability of a fixed position, they were unwilling to identify themselves too much in public with a group whose stature in the Thirties was undecided. Woollcott, the one with most to gain from the association and the one whose extremes of sentiment would be most likely to produce roseate hindsight, also deferred writing about the subject, except to say in a letter to John

Peter Toohey shortly before he died, 'I should enjoy seeing just once more those old chums that I still dislike with a waning intensity.' Parker recalled 'that not particularly brave little band that hid its nakedness of heart and mind under the out-of-date garment of a sense of humor.'"

Continuing the tradition today in the Oak Room Cabaret, the imperishable songs of Broadway are performed and preserved for future generations. Each evening in the lobby, Broadway music resonates. And in-house guests may view film versions of popular Broadway musicals via the closed-circuit TV system.

Long after the glory days of Dorothy Parker, John F. Kennedy said, "When I was growing up, I had three wishes—I wanted to be a Lindbergh-type hero, learn Chinese, and become a member of the Algonquin Round Table." In 2002 the Algonquin celebrated its 100th anniversary and introduced a special "writer's rate" in honor of the occasion.

The **Plaza Hotel** at Fifth Avenue and 59th Street, has had a varied history. The building of the present Plaza started in 1905, after the demolition of an earlier Plaza Hotel on the same site. Construction took two years, the interior decoration and furniture was French, and it was intended to be the most luxurious hotel in the world.

At the beginning, it was used primarily as a town home for people who had houses elsewhere; the Vanderbilts were the first residents. F. Scott and Zelda Fitzgerald also lived there (Zelda is supposed to have danced naked in the fountain outside), and very many distinguished theatrical and artistic personalities were associated with it. George M. Cohan held court in the Oak Room; Enrico Caruso was so infuriated by the humming of an electric clock that he is said to have destroyed it with a knife. Mrs. Patrick Campbell stayed there on her first visit to the United States for her performances in *Hedda Gabler*. She smoked a cigarette in the Palm Court, causing a minor scandal. The Beatles stayed there for six days in 1964; Frank Lloyd Wright stayed for six years during the construction of the Guggenheim Museum, which he designed.

It has changed hands many times; Donald Trump and Conrad Hilton were among the better-known owners. It last sold for three hundred and twenty-five million dollars in 1995.

The Plaza has been used as a locale for countless films. Some of the most noteworthy are: *Barefoot in the Park*, *Funny Girl*, *Plaza Suite*, *Arthur*, *Crocodile Dundee*, and *Sleepless in Seattle*. The hotel publicity suggests that it has featured in more than three hundred films. *Arthur*, of course, starred the late Dudley Moore in what was to become one of his biggest successes in America. The film also starred Sir John Gielgud, who became almost more famous in America for his role as the butler than for any other. When he died, a headline in a New York paper read "Butler in Dudley Moore film dies."

In 1955 *Eloise at the Plaza*, written by Kay Thompson and illustrated by Hilary Knight, was published, and a painting of the imaginary six-year-old heroine hung in the lobby, until it was stolen in 1960. The present painting of *Eloise* (by Hilary Knight) dates from 1964. The book is still extremely popular, as are the subsequent stories about Eloise. It is still sold in the hotel's gift shop and Hilary Knight often drops by to do book signings. In New York, Eloise is as famous as Alice in Wonderland. It is unusual that an actress created such a memorable book, and one that lives on well after the reputation and name of its creator.

Truman Capote threw the 1966 Black and White Ball in the Grand Ballroom. Guests included Frank Sinatra and Mia Farrow (then just married), Vivien Leigh, Lauren Bacall, Steven Sondheim, and Andy Warhol. The Oyster Bar, opened at the end of 1969, was patterned after an English pub, and with its Edwardian-era murals quickly became a favorite of New Yorkers.

Up to the 1970s there was the famed Persian Room, situated just off the front lobby at the Fifth Avenue entrance. It was where the top cabaret stars of the world performed before a glamorous and glittering audience. Eartha Kitt and Sacha Distel sang there, as did many European stars who crossed the Atlantic to appear there. Most other cabaret rooms at that time featured American artists, so the Persian Room was unique in presenting the crème de la crème of overseas nightclub performers.

The American playwright, Neil Simon, set one of his plays in a suite there and called it *Plaza Suite*—where he celebrated the play's opening night. It was where Mick Jagger celebrated his 50th birthday bash, down in a special banquet room in the hotel's subterranean kitchens. The Plaza is where Michael Douglas and Catherine Zeta-Jones were married in lavish style, where Donald Trump first invited his then wife to re-decorate, where Liza Minnelli grew up, and where Eloise acted up. It's also where all those kings and queens stay when visiting the United Nations. Mrs. Patrick Campbell started the popularity of the hotel for visiting British thespians.

Just down the street is **Wyndhams** at 42 West 58th Street. It was a favorite of Alec Guinness and is very low-key compared to the glossy Plaza opposite. It has lovely interior decorated rooms, and is the home of many British actors such as Maggie Smith and Antony Sher. While acting in the play *Stanley* Sher was writing a novel. He called it *The Feast* and it was about Africa, the theater, and himself. In his biography he said he wrote from about 5 a.m. to 5 p.m. each day, sleeping in the hours left over. To read about his daily existence in New York, you realize that he loved the city, and the sheer energy and buzz of New York. Most British theater people agree that the excitement of Broadway is contagious.

Sher finished his book and after the run of *Stanley* he returned to England. He subsequently won the *Evening Standard* award for Best Actor (as Richard III), the Laurence Olivier best actor award (for *Stanley* and *Richard III*), Peter Sellers' *Evening Standard* film award (*Mrs. Brown*) Omnibus BBC 1997, was made an Honorary Doctor of Letters, and was knighted in 2000.

The **Waldorf Astoria** is still as gracious as ever. No visit to New York would be complete without a stop to see this hotel at 301 Park Avenue. Here is one of the all-time great theatrical hotels where the legendary Cole Porter lived—his piano used to be played in the Peacock Alley off the main lobby—as well as dozens of famous stars. The Duke and Duchess of Windsor lived for a time in the Waldorf Towers. So much has been noted in actors' biographies, it is difficult to name one or two, without leaving out your favorite star. In the foyer, just off the main lobby, you can see Cole Porter's piano which is still played by the resident pianist at cocktail hour. When unemployed and down, you can always feel the past sitting in Peacock Alley sipping a martini. Most everyone did it at some time or another. Often celebrities meet for a drink there and at any given time you might have met Ginger Rogers, Fred Astaire, Gene Kelly, Noël Coward, or Ivor Novello.

A word here about Cole Porter—and his lifestyle. The lyrics of Cole Porter remind us of the glamorous style he and his contemporaries lived in when they were in New York. If he wasn't traveling to Europe, staying in Venice, he was at the Waldorf Astoria.

When Noël Coward was asked to list things that had style he included any Cole Porter song. Coward understood as a playwright how written words should be performed. Elsa Maxwell, the famous party giver, was a close friend of Porter and he wrote one of his best songs for her birthday, "I'm dining with Elsa."

He wrote he was dining with Elsa and her ninety-nine most intimate friends. She gave parties in Paris, Venice, London, and of course New York. She said her job was to entertain the rich. When the Waldorf Astoria first opened, they offered her a free apartment in return for establishing the hotel as "the" place to be. They also gave Cole Porter his penthouse at a small fee for the same reason. People like Elsa and Cole formed the elite society circle which centred around them. She knew everyone. She was never boring and most of her guests found her entertaining.

The city of Venice had hired her to promote the Lido and so she and Cole Porter and his millionaire wife went there for the summer in 1923.

When Cole returned to New York he put the district of Harlem on the map. During the 1930s and '40s Harlem was where white folks, the café society, went to hear jazz. The Cotton Club became famous and it was the place to go after the theater. Cole Porter and his wife Linda were Broadway celebrities after his success with *Anything Goes*. Their lifestyle was written up in all the papers. Cole's songs had everyone dancing to his music.

Hollywood wanted him, but Cole stayed home at the Waldorf to write. Later on he met Moss Hart, the playwright. They went on a world cruise with their wives and he took his own piano. They were known as "Miss Linda and her gentlemen." It was on this cruise they wrote the show *Jubilee* and Cole composed "Begin the Beguine." Finally he did go to Hollywood. Sophisticated New Yorkers, including Dorothy Parker, considered the place a joke, even though she also wrote for the films. Hollywood loved Cole Porter and he was a great success, but Linda did not and she left him to return to New York.

When the story of his life was filmed (*Night and Day*, with Cary Grant in the role), they left out that he was a homosexual, although married to an extremely wealthy woman, and played down his wealth and lifestyle. He had become a living legend. They invited guests such as CBS chairmen William Paley, playwright Robert Sherwood, and Charlie Chaplin to their lavish dinners. He went to see Coward's play *Quadrille* with the Lunts and became a friend to all the top theater and film celebrities of that age, as well as to composers, writers, and musicians.

A rather big contrast to the Waldorf Astoria is the bohemian **Hotel Chelsea**, at 222 West 23rd Street, between Seventh and Eighth Avenues. The hotel first opened in the 1880s when 23rd Street was the heart of the theater district. It was built is 1884 as an apartment house, but in 1905 it became a hotel. As the theater district slowly moved up town from Astor Place, 23rd Street was the equivalent of what the Times Square area is now. Many theater people stayed here, and writers such as Vladimir Nabokov and later Arthur Miller, who called it the only hotel without class distinctions. It is now a decaying Edwardian building which has obviously seen better days. Bob Dylan wrote a song about it and Dylan Thomas spent his last days there. One night in November 1953 when he was in New York for a lecture tour of the States, he fell into an alcoholic stupor and collapsed at the nearby White Horse Tavern. He was taken to St. Vincent's Hospital, where he died.

Another alcoholic writer, Brendan Behan, stayed at the hotel, and in his book *Brendan Behan's New York* he requested that the owner of the hotel leave a space for a memorial plaque after his death outside the front door, where several others were already in place. After his death several years later, the plaque was installed and it is still there to this day. Jimi Hendrix, Janis Joplin, and the Grateful Dead all stayed here, as did Mark Twain. It is interesting to note that the hotel concierge says that Arthur C. Clarke wrote the book *2001: A Space Odyssey* while staying at the hotel.

Some British may remember Edie Sidgwick, the close companion of Andy Warhol, who lived in a studio apartment here. The film *The Chelsea Girls* was made here. The whole area around the hotel makes an interesting daytime walk, and further south at 17 West 16th Street is the home of Margaret Sanger, one of the pioneers of birth control. Her house, which for fifty years was the headquarters of her Clinical Research Bureau, is now painted purple with a Greek-pillared front doorway.

The **Edison Hotel** on West 47th Street is historically connected with Broadway. On its completion in 1936 the electricity was switched on by remote control by Mr. Edison himself from his home in New Jersey. It was the first electricity in New York and lit up Broadway and Times Square with electric light. The Art Deco designs in the lobby still stand, and it is worth a visit to see the kind of place that featured in the early movies and was the home of many British thespians working in the theater district in those times.

These days British actors who are in a Broadway play usually wait for the reviews to come out and learn whether the play is going to run before they begin to contemplate moving from a hotel into an apartment. During rehearsals it is easier to live in a hotel where there is always room service and you can order dinner at midnight if necessary. New York hotel staff are used to unusual demands, especially when there are actors resident.

3

The Players Club

Just as London has the Garrick Club, the Groucho Club and the Chelsea Arts Club, where actors, directors, and writers gather, New York has the Players, the Lambs, and the Friars. Any visitor to London would be fortunate to be issued an invitation to the Garrick Club; the same applies to **The Players** in New York. It is part of a New York tradition to attend a "Roast" at the Friars Club, and many an actor has been honored with a dinner at the Players, and then been able to watch a performance on the small stage at the end of the dining room. Sir John Gielgud said the Players was his second home when he was working on Broadway.

The Players is in downtown New York on the south side of Gramercy Park, in the center of which stands a full-length bronze statue of Edwin Booth as Hamlet on top of a granite pedestal. The club has a unique library of books about thespians and records of most of New York's theater history, including famous first nights with the great names of British legends on Broadway, from Henry Irving, Ellen Terry, and Laurence Olivier to the present day.

Lynn Redgrave became the first woman president of the club early in the 1990s for a brief time while she was in New York.

Step down to the entrance of No. 16 Gramercy Park, beneath a covered stone loggia from which project immense wrought-iron, Renaissance-style working gas lanterns, and enter the well-preserved 19th-century world of Edwin Booth.

The greatest American actor of his time, Booth bought the 1845 Gothic Revival-style house in early 1888 and commissioned architect Stanford White to transform it into a clubhouse suitable, in Booth's words, for "social intercourse between the representative members of the Dramatic profession, and of the kindred professions of Literature, Painting, Sculpture, and Music, and the Patrons of the Arts . . ." Here is an extract from Dan Moore's history of the Players:

> The Players opened as a club at midnight on New Year's Eve in 1888, and for more than a century it has fulfilled not only that goal but another objective set forth by Booth at the same time, ". . . the creation of a library relating especially to the history of the American Stage and the preservation of pictures, bills of the play, photographs, and curiosities, connected with such history."

From the foyer of the clubhouse, the dark-wood stairway is open to the fifth-floor skylight, and its ornately carved mahogany newel posts begin with a spotlighted bust of Shakespeare. Down a few steps and through the glass doors is the Grill Room, where several generations of actors, artists, writers, and others have gathered for conversation and refreshment. A focal point is the table where Samuel L. Clemens (Mark Twain) often shot pool with other founders of the club. His pool cue is displayed over his portrait above the fireplace, as are those of Frank Morgan, Franklin Pierce Adams, and others.

Artworks on every wall of the Grill Room include Marshall Goodman's watercolor of the club's past presidents, including British actor Michael Allinson. Here, too, are Norman Rockwell's portrait of Charles Coburn, John Barrymore's watercolors of the sets of *Hamlet*, James Cagney's drawing of Roland Winters, Thomas Nast's Tammany Tiger, and Al Hirschfeld's drawing of Edwin Booth (the only one he has ever done of an actor who wasn't alive when he drew it).

Near the Grill Room is the so-called Sarah Bernhardt Room, a tiny ancient elevator still in use in which the great actress became trapped for an hour or so one evening in 1911 while visiting the club as a guest. Art treasures line the wall space along the entire expanse of the building's open stairway. Leading up the entrance staircase to the Great Hall are portraits of John Henry Wallack, Edwin Forrest, and many others.

The Great Hall, on the first floor of The Players, is dominated by a massive fireplace designed by Stanford White to incorporate the club's seal with its masks of comedy and tragedy. Over the fireplace mantel hangs a painting by Robert Sully of Edwin Booth's father, Junius Brutus Booth, made up as Hamlet.

It is in the Great Hall that Players and their guests gather for receptions preceding Thursday dinners, Tuesday special entertainment evenings, and traditional black-tie events such as Founders' Night, New Year's Eve, and the Pipe Nights, when great actors and others eminent in their fields are saluted for their work.

Paintings of the club's first president, Edwin Booth posing as Richelieu, and of its second president, actor Joseph Jefferson in *The Rivals*, face each other at the entrance to the Dining Room, and a picture of Booth as Hamlet dominates the wall opposite the fireplace at the head of the stairs.

The Sargent Room, at the north end of the Great Hall, features oil paintings of three of the club's founders by John Singer Sargent, the best-known American portrait artist of the Victorian age. A full-length study of Edwin Booth, hanging over the fireplace, is flanked by portraits of Lawrence Barrett on the left and Joseph Jefferson on the right. Just inside the room is the oak Savonarola throne-chair in which John Barrymore sat when he performed his great Hamlet in 1922, and above it is his portrait.

The Dining Room, to the south of the Great Hall, is where the club's major events take place. At the far end of the room is an informal stage used frequently for performances and play reading.

Along the stairway to the second floor are portraits of actresses such as Katharine Hepburn, Muriel Kirkland, and Beatrice Lillie, as well as James Montgomery Flagg's pencil sketch of Rosalind Russell. A tall 18th-century English oak-case clock stands on the landing, beside an interior window depicting the masks of comedy and tragedy.

Near the entrance to the Library stands a door bearing a plaque which reads: "In this room during the first three months of 1913 there met without permission the small committee of four or five which ultimately led to the formation of the Actors Equity Association."

The Library, officially named the Hampden-Booth Theater Library after its principal donors, now occupies what originally were two large rooms at the front of the second floor, each with its own fireplace and mantel of red African marble. Over one mantel is a quotation from *The Tempest*: "My library was dukedom large enough for me." Over the other is a quotation from *Titus Andronicus*: "Take choice of all my library."

In 1957, the Library was chartered by the State of New York as an educational institution, and two years later it officially opened its doors for the first time to qualified researchers and students of the theater. Today the Hampden-Booth Theater Library is considered the finest repository of theater references, art, and memorabilia of its kind. With a growing collection of books, manuscripts, photographs, prompt scripts, notebooks, and more than 50,000 plays and many old quartos of early dramatists it is historically impressive.

The Card Room, at the far end of the second floor hallway, is used for private functions and committee meetings. It displays the poker table said to have been used by Mark Twain, portraits of James Cagney and Douglas Fairbanks Sr., and a photograph of three Cyranos, Walter Hampden, José Ferrer, and Jimmy Durante.

At the top of the stairs to the third floor are cases containing costumes Edwin Booth wore as Iago, Othello, Richard III, Hamlet, Macbeth, and in other roles. And the life mask of Ellen Terry faces a photograph nearby of her great-nephew John Gielgud in his 1936 role as Hamlet.

The Booth Room, at the front of the third floor, was called by Booth his "nest among the treetops of Gramercy Park." This is the suite, a parlor and a bedroom, where he lived his final five years after the opening of The Players. The rooms have been left furnished as they were when he died in 1893 at age 59, including several of the pipes and cigars he loved so much. The gasolier hanging over the dining table in the parlor still works, and occasionally it is lit.

Here still are many of Booth's personal treasures, reminders of his great theatrical career and of his family tragedies. In the far corner of the parlor near a window is a painting of his first wife and great love, the beautiful actress Mary Devlin, who died so young after only three years of marriage. Beneath her portrait is a bookcase, atop which rest memorabilia such as the skull of Yorick which Booth saluted hundreds of times while playing Hamlet. The skull is said to be that of a horse thief who asked just before being hanged that his skull be forwarded to Booth's father, whom he admired.

Between the parlor windows, a bust of Shakespeare looks down over Booth's roll-top desk and over it is a copy of the legend on Shakespeare's tomb at Stratford. On the table are Booth's cigar case, a bronze casting of his daughter Edwina's hand in his, and the book of poetry by William Winter open to the page he was reading before he died.

In the bedroom are the actor's brass bed with its faded silk coverlet and its canopy of yellow satin, and beside it rest his slippers. Near the window is his Queen Anne-style ebony wood chaise, and at its foot sits the oak make-up case he took on his tours. Beneath the window is his dressing table, and against another wall is a Chippendale bureau. On the wall behind the chaise is a shadow-box tribute to Booth.

In this personal retreat, where the great actor lived out his last years and died, can be found his continuing spirit, the essence of his life. But Edwin Booth lives on to this day in every room and on every floor of the Players, the club he founded and loved.

John Gielgud said: "I have the happiest memories of the Players Club where dinners were given for me and for the Lunts also." Laurence Olivier, too, remembered it fondly.

4

The Lambs Club

The London Lambs held its first weekly dinner on October 16, 1869, at the Gaiety Restaurant. It thrived for ten years when "the Lambs grew into old sheep and strayed from the Fold. Some died. Some married." In the meantime, in 1874, one of their number, actor Henry J. Montague, came to New York on a professional engagement. Henry Montague cut a dapper figure about town. With good looks, a knack for light comedy, and plenty of opportunity in the emerging New York theater, he had a bright and promising future before him. He would found the New York Lambs.

The Lambs in New York traces its lineage to early 19th-century London. "In those far off days the home of Charles Lamb, essayist, critic and leader in London's literary life, was a rendezvous for luminaries in the world of arts and letters. Numbered among them were the men of that period's vigorous and thriving theater," writes Lewis Hardee, the club historian, who gave me this report. Charles and his sister, Mary Lamb, maintained a lively salon where could be found good conversation, good food, good drink, and good fellowship. In 1869 a small group of actors and men about town decided to form a private dinner club, a popular idea of the day. John Hare, a veteran actor, is credited with having conceived the club. Tradition has it that when debating the choice of a name for the new fraternity, someone recalled their happy visits to the Lambs' salon when invariably someone would exclaim, "Let's go 'round to the Lambs!" Thus, "The Lambs."

The New York of 1874 was a city bursting with energy, optimism, and a rapidly exploding population. In 1870 its population stood at a million; by the end of the century it would triple in size. It extended from the Battery to 59th Street, beyond which were farms and land then only just being eyed by developers. It was a city whose skyline was spiked with church steeples and the masts of tall ships. Horse-drawn omnibuses and carriages rattled noisily and dustily through the busy streets. It was the Gaslight Era, when women wore bustles, when great hordes of immigrants disembarked from fleets of ships from Europe, when whiskey went for 5 cents a glass. Many of the great landmarks of New York were making their appearance on the scene—the American Museum of Natural History, the Metropolitan Museum of Art, the Brooklyn Bridge, the Statue of Liberty. Elevated railroad lines were rising above the streets, spewing from overhead their hot cinders over First, Second, Third, Sixth, and Ninth Avenues.

By 1874 the theater district had migrated from the Wall Street area to Broadway between Union and Herald Squares. Theater fare was abundant and varied. J. Lester Wallack's Theater, at 13th and Broadway, boasted classy French and English farces; Tony Pastor's on 14th Street provided the best in variety entertainment; the last of the great minstrels were at Bryant's; and opera reigned on 14th Street at the Academy of Music. Harrigan and Hart offered Irish and German tenement humor at their various theaters. Booth's Theater, at the southeast corner of Sixth Avenue and 23rd Street, provided stars domestic and foreign, and of course, Shakespeare.

The Lambs is the oldest theatrical society in America. For over a hundred and twenty-three years it has been central to New York theater. Its fame is global. ASCAP and Actors Equity were conceived there. Since its founding in 1874 its membership has included actors, producers, playwrights, composers, directors, and lovers of theater in general. Its roster of members reads like a *Who's Who* in the entertainment world—George M. Cohan, Al Jolson, John Philip Sousa, Victor Herbert, Will Rogers, David Belasco, W.C. Fields, Walter Cronkite, Eugene O'Neill, Irving Berlin, Oscar Hammerstein II, Sigmund Romberg, Alan J. Lerner and Frederick Loewe, Cecil B. De Mille, Douglas Fairbanks, Eddie Foy, both Sr. and Jr., Bert Lahr, Bert Wheeler, Fred Astaire, and Spencer Tracy, to name a few. Honorary members have included Col. Charles Lindbergh, Hon. Thomas E. Dewey, Dwight

D. Eisenhower, and John Wayne. Richard L. Charles, actor and publisher, is the incumbent Shepherd of the Lambs. His wife, Joyce Randolph (Trixie of TV's *The Honeymooners* fame) is a regular. Shepherd Emeritus Tom Dillon is President of the Actors' Fund of America.

As the nation goes, so goes Broadway; as Broadway goes, so goes the Lambs. The history of this great club has been directly connected to Broadway, the New York theater from which it sprang, and like Broadway, its fortunes have had many ups and downs. As Broadway grew from a fledgling, clumsy business to a dynamic industry, so did the Lambs; as Broadway has had its triumphs and tragedies, so has the Lambs. Their destinies were linked at birth.

At Christmas time 1874 George McLean hosted a supper party for his theater friends at the Blue Room of fashionable Delmonico's Restaurant. His guests were Arthur Wallack, Henry J. Montague, Harry Beckett, and Edward Arnott. The evening proved so agreeable that it was decided to meet on a regular monthly basis. After the festivities had gone on for nearly two and a half years, Henry Montague suggested that the little club be called The Lambs, after the club in London to which he had belonged.

Montague's hand is all over the place, and it was through his influence that nomenclature and traditions of the London Lambs were adopted in America. "The Lambs" was chosen as the club name, the vice-president was called "The Boy," the clubhouse "The Fold," and outings or excursions were "Washes." Montague was elected its first "Shepherd," or president.

The original membership of twelve was increased "by sevens," and by 1887 the club could boast a membership of sixty. On May 10 of that year it was incorporated under the laws of the State of New York. The Founding Council numbered five: John A. Stow, Henry A. Barclay, George W. Walker, Edmund M. Holland, and John A. Balestier. The Certificate of Incorporation laid out its aims and ideals, which continue to this day:

> The particular business and object of such Society or Club is the bringing together of its members for the purpose of social recreation and the cultivation of musical, literary and artistic talent, including the creation and maintenance of funds for the benefit of persons engaged professionally in drama, music, authorship, and the fine arts, who shall be in need of financial aid or assistance, to be disbursed in the discretion of the Council of the Club.

Following the organizational supper at Delmonico's, there were two gatherings at the Maison Doree Hotel, after which meetings were held at the Union Square Hotel. The next move was to the second floor of 848 Broadway, "The Matchbox," a tiny saloon jammed in next to Wallack's Theater. Its nickname gives us a vivid picture of its state or condition. The Lambs then leased an entire floor of nearby Monument House. After a year it was noted that the entire assets of the club amounted to the sum of $80.40, and the Lambs was on the move again, to 19 East 16th Street.

Maurice Barrymore, father of John, almost made the Lambs Club his home (as did John Drew The Players). There he could fend off bores. "Don't you recognise me, Mr. Barrymore?" "I didn't at first, but when you didn't buy I knew you right away." Told by a friend he must see E.H. Southern's *Hamlet*, he replied, "My boy, I don't encourage vice."

At the close of the old century men of great prestige had been added to The Lambs membership, including the celebrated actor, Sir Henry Irving, General Horace Porter of Civil War fame, Charles A. Dana, and Dion Bouccicault. The fortunes of the club began to soar. By 1895 it was debt-free with a membership of 272 and excited with plans for the future. In 1897 a long-held dream was realized, to have a "roof controlled by the club." The site was 70 West 36th Street (presently occupied by Keene's Chop House).

But the Lambs has always been more than a social club, and through the years has made significant contributions to community service and cultural life. During World War I Lambs provided entertainment for the troops. A generous bequest in 1923 by Percy Williams, Broadway producer and former Treasurer of the Club, established his estate at East Islip, Long Island, as a home for retired actors and actresses. The home was later incorporated in the Actors' Fund Home in Englewood, New Jersey.

In 1975 the building was sold, its works of art and memorabilia sold or placed in storage. "We're poor little lambs who have gone astray, baa, baa, baa . . ."—the song which concludes many Lambs events—seemed bitterly appropriate.

Once again The Lambs ordered new stationery, and the fold relocated within the Lotos Club at 5 East 66th Street. The Lotos, however, with its dignified, Ionic-columned rooms, its elegant crystal chandeliers and Chippendale dining chairs, proved uncongenial to the rambunctious Lambs. Also, it was uptown on the East Side and far from the action. In the opinion of some despairing members, the club should be disbanded. But a group of diehards refused to allow an end to an institution with so rich a history and traditions, and ripe with promise. In 1997 a move was made to the present location at 3 West 51st Street.

The old traditions continue. Throughout the year the Lambs presents variety shows, plays, musicals, and other entertainments. The weekly Happy Hour features impromptu Low Jinks, and conclude with the traditional joining of hands to sing "Baa, Baa, Baa." Annual outings are held at the Actors' Fund Home. In its private rooms members enjoy pool, socializing, or rehearsing for auditions. The Foundation continues its important work.

5

The Friars Club

For years, women were not permitted to enter the interior of the Friars Monastery. At the Clubhouse on 48th Street, there was a small cubicle at the entrance of the building and it was not unusual to see women performers like Gracie Allen (Burns and Allen), Mary Livingston Benny, and Eva Sully (Block and Sully), sitting in the little reception area waiting for their husbands, George Burns, Jack Benny, and Jesse Block, three close friends, to join them as they left the club. Subsequently, on 56th Street and in the present Monastery, the rules have been changed to permit women in the Clubhouse after 4 p.m.

A new era was welcomed at the New York Friars in 1988 with the admission of women as full-fledged members. Liza Minnelli was the first woman to apply for membership and the first admitted. She was followed by such shining stars as Carol Burnett, Phyllis Diller, Edie Gormé, Anjelica Huston, Martha Raye, Joan Rivers, Brooke Shields, Dinah Shore, Barbara Sinatra, Barbra Streisand, and Elizabeth Taylor. Soon after gaining admittance, Rivers joked that "the Club is so nice, I'm

thinking of making it an all-women's organisation."
There have been many changes since the club's
inception in 1904, but through the century it has
remained devoted to the original purpose of
providing a warm and comfortable environment
for the entertainment industry. Of the club's 1,400
members, two-thirds must be involved in show
business-related activities. The remaining one-
third of the membership consists of prominent
individuals from the corporate world.

The club traces its beginnings back to a group of
theatrical publicists who called a meeting of the
Press Agents' Association at Browne's Chop House.
They were concerned about the huge amount of
complimentary tickets being distributed by
theaters, as well as other abuses that threatened the
stability of their industry. Meeting each Friday, the
group eventually reached agreements with producers, managers, and box office treasurers to
correct the situation. Two years later, at another
meeting in Keene's Chop House, the scope of the
organization was expanded to include press agents
from around the country along with a wider
spectrum of the theatrical industry.

Many British performers working on Broadway
are invited to dinner at the Friars. In the past they
have rubbed shoulders with Frank Sinatra, Yul
Brynner, Elizabeth Taylor, and Mike Todd.
Gathered each day in this five-story brownstone
building at 57 East 55th Street are the best and
brightest of show business, the world's top

headliners telling tales among themselves while enjoying the club's excellent facilities, exquisite surroundings, and superb cuisine.

In a tradition that started at the turn of the century under the leadership of George M. Cohan, the Friars Club has attracted the elite of show business as well as distinguished industry leaders through the years. The exalted position of Abbot has been held by such legends as George M. Cohan, George Jessel, Mike Todd, Milton Berle, Joe E. Lewis, Ed Sullivan, and Frank Sinatra.

The greatest songwriter of all time, Irving Berlin, wrote "Alexander's Ragtime Band" for the first Friars Frolic in 1911. Other early members included heavyweight champions Jack "Manassa Mauler" Dempsey and Gentleman Jim Corbett.

As important as their dedication to entertaining the world is the devotion of Friars members to charitable causes. Those in show business are givers, not takers, and the club's support of humanitarian causes has always been achieved with modesty. Under the auspices of the Sunshine Committee, the Friars Club is heavily involved in caring for the less fortunate. It subsidizes a traveling troupe of performers that entertains at hospitals and senior citizens' homes. Its annual Christmas/Channukah film party is attended by 1,500 underprivileged children. Each attendee receives a shopping bag filled with toys, games, clothing, and merchandise.

In addition, hundreds of thousands of dollars are raised by the Friars Foundation, the charitable arm of the New York Friars Club, and these funds are distributed to performing arts institutions and colleges. Members on an individual basis probably have done more for charitable causes than any other association.

They are fierce in their dedication to the sick and the needy, and throughout their long and honorable history the Friars have, through their Celebrity Luncheons, Roasts, and Testimonial Dinners, raised millions of dollars for worthy causes. The then Abbot Frank Sinatra said, "Their continuous good work for charity rather than their great triumphs on the stages of the world is the true glory of this band of earthly angels known as the New York Friars."

The City of New York has honored the Friars Club and its members on two occasions for its contributions to the world of entertainment and its dedication to the welfare of its citizens. The first honor was a statue of Abbot George M. Cohan which was erected in New York's Times Square on Broadway and 47th Street. In 1983, on the steps of City Hall, Mayor Edward I. Koch presented the club its second honor with a "Certificate of Appreciation" for its outstanding contribution to New York City and the community.

At this time the name Friars was adopted to express the more fraternal purpose of the organization. Frederick F. Schrader is credited with suggesting the name. The weekly Friday meetings were held at the Hotel Hermitage until the Friars took possession of their first building at 107 West 45th Street. The Clubhouse, which came to be known the Hermitage, was formally opened May 9, 1908. Charles Emerson Cook was named the club's second Abbot, succeeding Wells Hawks.

The celebrated tradition of honoring personalities had already begun. In 1907 Victor Herbert, who was the guest of honor at a dinner, sang his speech "Here's to the Friars" and it has been the Friars' Anthem ever since. Herbert wrote the music and Charles Emerson Cook penned the words.

The "Friars Frolics" were the Galas of the Friars before the annual Testimonial Dinners and Celebrity Roasts became the attraction they are now. Abbot George M. Cohan assembled a star-studded cast for the Frolics of 1916. The cast featured Cohan, then the King of Broadway, Will Rogers, Willie Collier, De Wolf Hopper, Irving Berlin, the first of the internationally known female impersonators, Julian Eltinge, the legendary minstrel showman, Lew Dockstader, and Victor Herbert and his Orchestra. "The Frolics" played 16 cities in 14 days. It premiered on a Sunday night at New York's New Amsterdam Theater, and on Monday a matinée was played in Philadelphia and a special command performance took place later that same night in Washington, D.C., for President Woodrow Wilson on the stage of the old Ford Theater where Lincoln was shot.

When the curtain came down, President Wilson went backstage to personally thank the cast. Right there and then, Abbot Cohan introduced a resolution which was carried unanimously electing President Woodrow Wilson as the first honorary member, and he accepted the gesture most graciously.

George M. Cohan, one of America's great songwriters and entertainers, was installed as Abbot in 1912. With the exception of two years, 1920 and 1927, it was a post he held through 1932. With the proceeds of "The Frolics" road tour, Cohan spurred the drive to build a new Clubhouse on West 48th Street, and he hired architect Harry Alan Jacobs to design the new building for the Friars Club. The style of the exterior was Tudor Gothic. The large windows on the second floor frankly expressed the dignified banquet hall, as it was the chief feature of the building. Here, the Friars held their entertainment. Naturally, because the club members belonged mostly to the theatrical profession, this room was the center of the entire plan, where the Friars continued to perform their sketches, impromptu entertainment and their famous Testimonial Dinners for members and friends.

The new Monastery at 106 West 48th Street was officially opened on May 22, 1916, with fitting pomp and ceremony. The Abbot George M. Cohan led the procession from the old Monastery to the new quarters, where he broke a bottle of sparkling American wine on the cornerstone and declared, "I dedicate our Friars Club to Art, Literature and

Good Fellowship." More than 500 Friars attended the opening banquet and the program that evening included performances by legendary stars of the day.

The building was considered to be the most handsome Clubhouse in New York City, modern in every detail while still retaining the intimate characteristics so essential to a fraternal group. The club continued to prosper. On May 1, 1916, there were 658 active members, 292 lay members, 258 non-residents and four members in the military service. The total membership represented an increase of 282 in one year.

The annual "Frolics", staged in the Grand Hall of the Monastery, played before standing-room only audiences. Among those celebrated at various dinners were Mayor Jimmy Walker, Governor Alfred E. Smith, Lee Shubert, Oscar Hammerstein, George M. Cohan, David Belasco, Irving Berlin, John Ringling, Mary Pickford and Douglas Fairbanks, and Enrico Caruso. The first woman honored by the Friars was Sophie Tucker in 1953. No other club has been as successful in attracting such a distinguished company of intellectual and notable personalities at its functions.

The Friars boasts of two members, George M. Cohan and Irving Berlin, who were honored by presidents of the United States with the Congressional Medal of Honor. Cohan wrote the famed World War I song, "Over There" in the original Friars Clubhouse.

Hard times struck the Friars, and the whole of the world, in 1932. The depression, the demise of vaudeville, and a mass trek westward to Hollywood by many stars seeking work in the film industry, decimated the ranks of Friars. The trade paper, *Variety*, reported an incident that took place during those years of financial strain. A produce purveyor who was owed some $600 by the Friars went to court and obtained a judgment to have a padlock placed on the Monastery until he got paid. Harry Hershfield, a great humorist of this time, was the Treasurer and he appealed to the court to have the padlock removed. When the Judge suggested to Hershfield that members' dues be raised, Hershfield replied, "The Members don't want to owe any more money." Somehow, the money was raised and the padlock was removed.

Eventually, the 48th Street Clubhouse was abandoned, although a hard core of the membership continued to operate the organization at various sites, first in the Lindy's building at 51st Street and Broadway and later at the Hotel Edison. It wasn't until 1948 that a new home was found when then Abbot Milton Berle and Treasurer-Legal Secretary Louis P. Randell negotiated for the Clubhouse at 128 West 56th Street.

In 1956, Abbot Emeritus Milton Berle, Abbot Joe E. Lewis, Dean Harry Delf, and the members decided to purchase another new Clubhouse. The building they selected is the present Headquarters at 57 East 55th Street, and this beautifully designed structure has remained the home of the Friars ever since.

Known from 1937 as "The Martin Erdmann Residence", a five-story English Renaissance house, it is considered by contemporary critics to be a capable and clever work of architecture. The decade in which it was erected was one of tremendous building activity on the part of wealthy merchants, manufacturers, and bankers. Andrew Carnegie, William Payne Whitney, the Astors, F.W. Woolworth, and many others undertook the task of building palatial residences. Occasionally, the result was a noble monument to the derivative genius of some American architect trained in Europe and given freedom to create. Such was undoubtedly the case with the Erdmann residence.

The late Mr. Martin Erdmann was a bachelor, and a collector of English mezzotints, who engaged the architectural firm of Taylor and Levi in 1908 to build a home for himself and his valuable art collection. He purchased two plots of ground on East 55th Street, each having a frontage of sixteen-and-one-half feet. The plots were occupied by a four-story brownstone house which was torn down to make room for the new structure. The location was considered to be a fine residential section, which had been guaranteed a dignified development by the inclusion of restrictive clauses in all of the property deeds, forbidding the establishments of such nuisances as livery stables, breweries, tanneries, forges or blacksmith shops, glue factories, ink or vitriol manufacturies, and other similar trades of equally noisome character. These restrictions still remain in the property deed acquired by the Friars Club.

The move to the new Clubhouse marked the beginning of the club's most successful era. Major alterations have been made from the basement to the roof to make the Clubhouse what it is today. The first floor contains the main dining room and the Round-the-World bar, renamed the William B. Williams lounge in memory of the former Dean. The second floor houses the Milton Berle Room and the Joe E. Lewis Bar, while the third floor consists of the Ed Sullivan Room, the Frank Sinatra Room, and the George Burns Cardroom. The Billiard Room named after former Dean Harry Delf and the Barber Shop are on the fourth floor. The fifth floor contains the well-equipped Health Club, named after former Dean Buddy Howe.

It has been the tradition of the Friars Club to honor its deceased members with plaques on the backs of the chairs in the main dining room. Periodically the names are changed but the chairs with the illustrious names remain. Among past Friars whose names have been immortalized are: Edward F. Albee, Yul Brynner, Eddie Cantor, Bing Crosby, Jimmy Durante, Douglas Fairbanks, W.C. Fields, Oscar Hammerstein, George Jessel, Harry Hershfield, Al Jolson, Ted Lewis, Edward R. Murrow, Will Rogers, Lee Shubert, Joe Smith, Ed Sullivan, Mike Todd, Richard Tucker, James J. Walker, and Walter Winchell.

The Friars Club is considered to be one of the top-rated clubs in the country. The club is famous world-wide for its Celebrity Roasts and Testimonial Dinners honoring the stars of show business. The famed Celebrity Roast, which features the greats of the entertainment world taking their best barbs at a Guest of Honour, is the most imitated function throughout the country. Moreover, the format has been used on a number of television shows. The home of the Friars is situated in what is known to today's real estate brokers as a protected area. All around the Clubhouse are developments which preclude the possibility of the neighborhood becoming a blighted area. Within close proximity of the Rockefeller Center, Fifth, Park and Madison Avenues, and Central Park, they all guarantee that land values will remain high. For the most part, these developments have risen within the past one hundred years. Fifth Avenue, which a century ago was called Middle Road above Forty-Second Street, changed from country land to fashionable residential street and then to a fashionable business avenue. Central Park has lent prestige to the north-central section of Manhattan since its construction in 1857. The Friars Club, located close to the center of this favored area, benefits by the proximity of these great investments. With its distinguished past and promising future, it will remain an interesting and prominent edifice for many decades.

6

Early British Stars of Broadway

There are a few historic restaurants left in New York where early visiting actors would have dined during their stay in America. Rector's of course is long gone but it was where these legendary actors would have had receptions given for them. The Plaza Hotel was popular especially because afternoon tea was served in the Palm Court. Even to this day this is one custom that is not practiced by most Americans, as it still remains a very British habit. Most New Yorkers do not have afternoon tea, and it is regarded as rather quaint if you request it. You may get a cup of tea with a tea bag in it but don't expect cucumber sandwiches or scones or anything to eat at all. You could get by with a piece of pie or cheesecake, but forget scones or muffins. One wonders how these actors survived without afternoon tea!

It was as early as the 1830s that the British stars went to America: Charles Matthews (1832), William Macready (1826–49), Edmund Kean (1830), Charles Kemble and his daughter Fanny (1832), Charles Wyndham (1869), Oscar Wilde (1882, on a lecture tour), Forbes Robertson, Mr. and Mrs. Kendall,

Marie Tempest, Lillie Langtry, Herbert Beerbohm Tree (1882), and Henry Irving (1883, 1904). No company (or actor) was more important in the United States during the nineteenth century than Irving's company. They toured eight times playing most major cities, a total of two hundred and nine weeks. But the legitimate theater has not been the only attraction. Marie Lloyd, Vesta Tilley, and Harry Lauder (music-hall stars) all made tours in the United States.

As far back as 1820 Edmund Kean electrified American audiences, and besides being paid far more highly than any other performer had even been, he became an honorary Chief of the Huron Indians.

In 1849 there were the horrendous Astor Place riots in New York City, arising from simultaneous productions of *Macbeth*, with the title role being played by the visiting English actor William Macready at the Astor Place Theatre, and by his bitter rival Edwin Forrest at the Bowery. In the ensuing chaos twenty-two people were killed and thirty-six injured.

But in terms of audience enthusiasm and public excitement there is no event in U.S. theater history to compare with the visit of Charles Dickens in 1867/8 to present readings of his works. The scenes of hysteria at his performances, and the riots among people trying to get tickets, were more sensational than the wildest excesses of Beatlemania or the antics of the hyped-up fans of the latest pop megastar. Dickens was always devoted to the theater.

As a youth he spent much of his very limited pocket money on play-going and, but for a series of flukes of the kind that can channel and divert all our lives, he might well have pursued an acting rather than a writing career.

His meteoric success as an author in the U.K. was swiftly matched in the U.S. although his material rewards from the States were severely curtailed by the widespread piracy brought about by loose copyright laws. Before he was thirty the serialized chapters of his novels had come to have an addictive fascination for the public as strong as today's TV soap operas.

The death of Little Nell in *The Old Curiosity Shop* had a profound effect on Dickens himself, but even more on his readers, many of whom confessed to having been brought to uncontrollable tears. The Irish M.P. Daniel O'Connell was in a train when he read the chapter. He broke into sobs and flung the book from the carriage window, crying "He should not have done it." When the ship carrying copies of the last chapters of the story was approaching the pier at New York harbor, there were crowds on the waterfront shouting to those on board "Is Little Nell dead?"

By the time Dickens came to present his readings in the U.S.A. he was the most famous author and one of the most famous people in the world. He had begun readings from his works nearly fifteen years earlier, to raise funds for various charities.

They had been immensely successful and led to his touring the U.K. on his own account (despite the misgivings of some of his more snobbish friends who felt it was not quite "gentlemanly" for him to exhibit himself in this way); but quite apart from enjoying the financial benefits, Dickens was moved by a kind of response from the public that no author had ever enjoyed before. It was warm, it was tangible, and it was immediate. He could not resist it, despite the sapping of his strength and the damage to his health.

When he arrived in the States there were extraordinary scenes as people strove to get tickets. Days before sales began there were hundreds camping in the streets with blankets and mattresses in the bitter winter weather, and waiters from neighboring restaurants and bars providing a running food and drinks service. Riots broke out only partly controlled by club-wielding police when speculators tried to infiltrate the line-up. Touts acquired and sold tickets at scores of times their face value.

Dickens gave seventy-six performances and they produced unprecedented demonstrations of enthusiasm, with cheers and tears and standing ovations everywhere; but on Dickens himself they imposed a heavy toll. He had constantly to seek medical help and traveled with a chest of medications including laudanum and digitalis. His manager had often to revive him with brandy during the intermission and sometimes he would lie prostrate on a sofa for half an hour at the end of the evening. Even so, he never missed a performance, and, before his last reading in New York, managed to attend and speak at a huge farewell banquet at Delmonico's. When he embarked on the ship that was to carry him back to England, a whole convoy of tugs, steamboats, and police tenders followed it down the Bay, saluting with whistles and cannons, Dickens himself meanwhile, standing on the deck, waving his hat on the end of his cane and shouting "Goodbye, God bless you, everyone."

Two British stars who also would have brought over their habit of afternoon tea were Gilbert and Sullivan, who arrived in New York in 1879 on the Cunard steamship, *Bothnia*. It is interesting to know the reason for their visit. The *Pirates of Penzance* was premiered there and Sullivan completed it when he was living on East 20th Street. Their main mission, however, was to stop their work from being illegally produced. Pirate copies of all their comic operas were being performed all over the country as copyright laws had still not been introduced in the United States at that time. For the *Pirates of Penzance* they were determined to beat the producer-pirates. Rehearsals were secret, none of the music was printed, and during the entire run the music was collected from the orchestra and locked in a safe each night. Unbelievably, Sullivan, in his hurry, had left some of his music in London and most of the songs for the first act. The show was to open in a month, and as steamship travel was slow, there was no time to send for them. So he rewrote all the songs from memory, and scored the entire opera, all in one month. Their comic operas were as popular and successful in America as in England.

In the golden era of transfers of British productions to New York, when Binkie Beaumont was still running the West End, there were many great performers who were tempted to stay in America and go to Hollywood. Some went for a short while but then returned home. Gladys Cooper was one star who did go to live in Hollywood, but regularly worked on both sides of the Atlantic, and returned to New York to appear in Enid Bagnold's *The Chalk Garden* in 1955, in which she also made her last stage appearance in London shortly before her death.

New York audiences were eager to see plays by British writers. They welcomed among others George Bernard Shaw, J.B. Priestley, Somerset Maugham, Terence Rattigan, and Noël Coward. However, these playwrights did not settle in the States but returned home after their plays were produced.

George Bernard Shaw wrote novels, drama, and music criticism for nine years before he became a successful playwright. It is well known that he was a vegetarian, which probably astounded New Yorker producers and actors as they were usually meat-eaters and steakhouses abounded on and around Broadway. Mrs. Patrick Campbell once attacked him and said, "Some day, Joey, you will

eat a pork chop and then God help all women."
Two of his plays were produced in New York in
the 1890s. His success came very quickly after
constant rejection in Britain, and finally he was
established, not only in New York but also in the
U.K. Richard Mansfield, an actor-manager, used to
boast that he had made Shaw a fortune. Most of
his plays opened in New York shortly after the
London openings, and it was only then that Shaw
became financially independent. Two of his plays
had their world premieres in New York, *Heartbreak House* and *St. Joan*, and then the Theater
Guild presented seven more.

Eugene O'Neill admired Shaw and wrote that his
own writing was influenced by him. Several other
U.S. playwrights also started to imitate Shavian
themes, including Edward Sheldon who wrote a
play called *Salvation Nell*. Shaw received an
Academy Award in 1938 for best screen adaptation
of his own play *Pygmalion*, starring Wendy Hiller
and Leslie Howard. However, one play, *Mrs.
Warren's Profession*, was viciously attacked and
called obscene by the New York press, the cast
even being put in jail for a short time, but the
ensuing publicity caused a surge at the box office
and Shaw became famous.

When Peggy Ashcroft went to New York in 1937
to play in *High Tor*, a verse play by Maxwell
Anderson, she found she had English friends in
town such as John Gielgud and Harry Andrews.
She met Ruth Gordon, Lillian Gish, and the rather

sad expatriate figure of Mrs. Patrick Campbell, then living in a little hotel on West 49th Street, and memorably compared by Alexander Woollcott to a "sinking ship firing on her rescuers." Peggy said:

I lived in an apartment block in Washington Square for six months on my own. I feel you either sink or swim in New York, and I sank. I never got used to the brilliant artificiality of New York and the fact that no one seemed to have homes, one always seemed to meet people in restaurants. Possibly the most memorable time I spent was with Edward Sheldon who was married to the actress Doris Keane, and who had in his day been a very popular playwright. He was blind, had been stricken with paralysis and lived in his apartment stretched out on a bier. Every day friends would come and read the paper to him, tell him all the latest theatrical gossip and read books to him. I joined in not out of pity but because I so much admired his stoicism and courage. He gave far more to his visitors than they could ever give to him.

But Peggy was not, and was never likely to become, a Broadway baby. Theatrically New York was much livelier in 1937 than it is today (there was Maurice Evans in *Richard II*, Helen Hayes in *Victoria Regina*, *Babes in Arms*, *You Can't Take it with You*, *Tobacco Road*) but the hype, the star worship, the belief that every new opening is an event of cosmic significance, that are endemic to Broadway, were miles removed from Peggy's fundamental belief in a theater of organic growth and familial closeness.

The best thing to happen to Peggy in New York was an invitation from her mentor and friend Sir John Gielgud to join him back in London to form a company inside a commercial framework.

Looking back, the golden era, the legend of Broadway really began in the 1920s, when Jack Buchanan, the British actor, starring in *Between the Devil* with Evelyn Laye and Adele Dixon, was hailed as "The King of Broadway."

7

Dorothy Parker and the Algonquin Round Table

Dorothy Parker was born Dorothy Rothschild on August 22, 1893, in West End, Monmouth County, a rather snobbish resort. Her father was in the garment business; he was also a Talmudic scholar who was entitled to and used the title of doctor. While his Jewish origin might have been a disadvantage socially, he made up for this with his wealth and good manners. His wife Eliza (née Marston) was of Scottish origin. She had been a schoolteacher in Scotland, but died when Dorothy was six years old. Her father remarried a religiously fanatical Protestant lady. Dorothy hated her father, who was a strict disciplinarian and dictatorial; she also hated her stepmother, a Christian fundamentalist who joined Dorothy's father in trying to indoctrinate Dorothy with religion.

There were few schools for Jewish children and none that her parents considered suitable, so she was sent to a Catholic convent school, where she was not unhappy, but her parents were invited to remove her, largely because of her irreverence in matters religious. After much deliberation on the part of her parents she was then enrolled in Miss Dana's School for Young Ladies in Morristown, New Jersey. She started there in the spring of 1906 and stayed until the fall of 1910. The school was a combination of finishing school and a college preparatory school; the curriculum was old-fashioned with an emphasis on Latin language and literature, French, mathematics and some science, English, art history and, inevitably, the Bible.

Dorothy was happy there, studied hard, and did well, but had no interest in games. She immersed herself particularly in the Latin authors; at this school she began to write short stories and verse and decided to make her living as a writer. When her years at school were finished she returned to live at her parents' New York house for a few months, then left home apparently to her parents' relief; her father gave her a small allowance. She moved into a boardinghouse on Broadway at 103rd Street, continued to write and had some of her work accepted by the New York magazine *World*. Her father's death in 1913 did not affect her particularly, and she did not attend his funeral.

In her boardinghouse home, she became acquainted with other writers and began to send her verses to magazines including *Vanity Fair*, at that time edited by Frank Crowninshield. She made a little money teaching children the piano; her main interest, however, remained writing, and when one of her poems was accepted by

Crowninshield, he arranged to meet her and gave her a job on *Vogue* magazine, a job which was poorly paid and involved fairly menial work which did not satisfy her one bit. However, Crowninshield later offered her a position at *Vanity Fair*, which covered society, theater, the arts, and literature. Its contributors included Gertrude Stein, D.H. Lawrence, H.G. Wells, T.S. Eliot, G.K. Chesterton, and Arnold Bennett, and as illustrators Henri Matisse, Raoul Dufy, and Marie Laurencin.

She was happier at *Vanity Fair*, which published her verse and prose pieces, and she collaborated with Crowninshield on his book *High Society*, supposedly a source of advice on how to get on in society; she also provided captions for the drawings in it. While working at the magazine she was active both professionally and socially, and met her future husband, Edwin Pond Parker II, who was an investment broker on Wall Street, a rich, well-connected, handsome, upper-crust individual whose only drawback was his fondness for whiskey, of which he drank a bottle or more every day. She was twenty-four, and hopelessly in love with Parker. In 1917, when America entered the war, he enlisted in the 33rd Ambulance Company as an ambulance driver; he and Dorothy married in June 1917 during his training, and in July he was sent overseas and was soon in action. He was severely wounded but survived, and at the end of the war was posted to the Rhineland with the occupying troops. He resumed his heavy drinking there, which continued after he was demobilized and returned to New York and to Dorothy in 1919. She was by then established in the "Vicious Circle," the Round Table at the Algonquin. He escorted her to the theater and to parties, and occasionally had lunch at the Algonquin Round Table, where he embarrassed Dorothy by his inability to join in the repartee or the literary conversations. She openly spoke of her contempt for him; the marriage was soon in effect over, although the official divorce was not obtained until 1928, on the grounds of Edwin's "cruelty" (his drinking).

The Algonquin already had a long history of literary association; Mark Twain, William Makepeace Thackeray, and Edgar Allan Poe had been among its patrons, as had many actors, members of the Barrymore family, Douglas Fairbanks, and John Drew. However, its current fame dates back to the trio of literary celebrities consisting of Robert Benchley, Robert Sherwood, and Dorothy Parker, who worked for Crowninshield at *Vanity Fair*, and who began to lunch together almost daily, usually at the Algonquin, which was close to their place of work. Since they were all, with the exception of Sherwood, poverty-stricken at the time, lunch was meager, consisting of scrambled eggs and coffee or hors d'oeuvres, never any of the more expensive entrées.

Other celebrated patrons included Alexander Woollcott, Franklin Adams, and Harold Ross, who during the war had been the editorial team of *Stars and Stripes*, the American armed forces' newspaper published in Paris. They also developed the habit of lunching at the Algonquin, as did other journalists and theater people. They were seated together by the manager of the restaurant, housed initially in the Pergola, then in the Rose Room, where the company was named "The Round Table" by a press agent, Murdock Pemberton.

Public relations people and publicists of various kinds took a keen interest in the goings-on at the Algonquin, and the legend fed upon itself. The hotel became the occasional destination of a host of illustrious names such as Noël Coward, Harpo Marx, Alfred Lunt, Lynn Fontanne, Lady Gregory (founder of the Abbey Theatre in Dublin), and George S. Kaufman, playwright and drama editor of the *New York Times*, Henry Miller, Paul Robeson, James Thurber, Richard Rodgers, and many others.

Regulars included music critics Bill Murray, Deems Taylor, columnist Heywood Broun, cartoonist Duffy of the Brooklyn *Daily Eagle*, and editors Crowninshield (*Vanity Fair*) and Art Samuels (*Harper's Bazaar*), Marc Connelly, a journalist/playwright who said that Dorothy Parker was the most riveting presence at the table.

Witticisms, some spontaneous, some no doubt prepared in advance, were the meat and drink of the Round Table. These people were highly competitive and their sallies were often at each others' expense or at the expense of occasional guests. They were not necessarily politically correct either. Samples include "Once there were two Jews—and now look." Variously attributed, but actually said by Robert Benchley after he had arrived at the Algonquin drenched from a rainstorm, was "Let's get out of these wet clothes and into a dry martini." Benchley again: "The trouble with me is I can't worry. Dammit, I try to worry and I can't." Alexander Woollcott, on being called by a critic the worst writer in America, said, "I'm potentially the best writer in America, but I never had anything to say." This self-deprecating style was shared by Benchley: "It took me fifteen years to discover that I had no talent for writing but I couldn't give it up because by that time I was famous."

Dorothy Parker took over as drama critic at *Vanity Fair* from the English humorist P.G. Wodehouse in April 1918 and wrote monthly critiques until March 1920 when she was fired, though she continued to contribute to the magazine. Her theater reviews were often far from kind. Her review of *Tolstoy's Redemption* at the Plymouth Theatre began, "I went into the Plymouth Theatre a comparatively young woman, and I staggered out of it, three hours later, twenty years older." Of a production of J.M. Barrie's *Dear Brutus* she wrote: "It made me weep—and I can't possibly enjoy a play more than that." Writing about the dramatization of Pierre Louys's novel *Aphrodite*: "The production is painfully lacking. Possibly this is due in great part to the fact that most of the feminine members of the cast were recruited from the Century Roof, where they were trained for emotional roles in ancient Egyptian dramas by a course of dancing around between tables, singing 'Smiles'. Another factor is the casting of Etienne Girardot as physician to the Queen of Egypt, in which role he wears much the same makeup that he used to in 'Charley's Aunt'." Of another play: "This play holds the season's record thus far, with a run of four evening performances and one matinee. By an odd coincidence it ran just five performances too many."

Dorothy Parker was at this point enjoying life tremendously, going with her friends to the theater, to speakeasies and to parties, being a celebrity, and for the first time really loving her job, being quoted in gossip columns both in the U.S. and abroad. She moved into a small rented apartment on West 57th Street in the same building as artist Neysa McMein who gave lots of parties.

All good things come to an end, however. The critical reviews tended to make enemies of playwrights, directors, producers, and theater-owners. One of the most powerful of these, Florenz Ziegfeld, was a close friend of Condé Nast, the proprietor of *Vanity Fair*, who ordered Frank Crowninshield to fire her. Crowninshield had no choice in the matter, so in January 1920 she was given two months' notice. At the Algonquin she told her friends about her dismissal; immediately Robert Benchley and Robert Sherwood decided to resign in protest. All three accordingly left the magazine in March.

Sherwood was the first to get another job, as film critic of *Life* magazine. He was able to arrange that Benchley and Dorothy Parker be hired as regular contributors to *Life*, Benchley to write occasional theater reviews and other pieces, and Dorothy to write a poem a week, but she also wrote for other magazines including the *Saturday Evening Post*. She now had a regular income and the freedom to write whatever she liked.

The Round Table continued in full bloom. Robert Sherwood had met Scott and Zelda Fitzgerald in Paris and introduced them at the Algonquin. Dorothy considered them "too ostentatious for words." Alexander Woollcott said of Dorothy that she was an odd combination of Little Nell and Lady Macbeth. He decided that the Round Table needed a weekend retreat, so he had a house built on Neshobe, a small island on a lake in Vermont. This was supposed to be for work and for fun and games. No work was done, however, and the place was little more than a re-creation of the Algonquin with lots of talk, escapades of various kinds, drinking, croquet, and cribbage. Benchley didn't like it, especially not the games nor the seven o'clock breakfasts, and went only once. It was here that Dorothy met Charles McArthur, a freelance journalist and one-time public relations adviser. They began an affair which continued in New York; the problem was that McArthur was incapable of being faithful to anyone, including Dorothy. On learning of his infidelities she became depressed and began to smoke and drink heavily for the first time.

The discovery that she was pregnant was a horrible shock; she decided to have an abortion which was performed in a hospital on the West Side of the city. Afterwards she became deeply depressed over McArthur's desertion of her and the subsequent abortion, and after an evening spent at a speakeasy, phoned to a nearby restaurant for some food. When the delivery boy came with the food, he found that Dorothy had slashed her wrists and was bleeding to death. She shouted to him to get a doctor, he ran and called an ambulance which took her immediately to the Columbia Presbyterian Hospital. There she had innumerable visitors, among them Robert Benchley, who told her to "snap out of it, you might as well live."

On leaving the hospital she resumed her heavy drinking and smoking, but till she had recovered from her depression she avoided being alone as much as possible. She was being cultivated by the rich and famous, including people like the Averell Harrimans and Jock Whitney. When she dined out, she usually ordered a steak and salad if her escort was paying, and had no interest in "gourmet food" or indeed in any food except as a necessity. She got up late in the morning and wandered down to the Algonquin for lunch. Afternoons were spent with friends, evenings often at one speakeasy or another. They preferred the Puncheon Club at 42 West 49th Street (later the 21 Club) where, however, she didn't drink much.

Harold Ross had founded the *New Yorker* magazine, and had announced that, among others, Dorothy Parker, George Kaufman, Alexander Woollcott, and Marc Connelly were advisory editors, without telling them in advance. Soon Dorothy was contributing to it the "Diary of a New York Lady" as well as occasional contributions to the *Smart Set* magazine, and collaborating with Charles Adams on a book of light verse called *Women I'm Not Married To: Men I'm Not Married To*. Although Benchley was the regular columnist, she occasionally replaced him in reviewing plays. She reviewed a play by Elmer Rice, and soon announced that she was going to co-write a play with him, to be called *Soft Music*.

The new play, by then called *Close Harmony*, after a try-out in Wilmington, moved to Broadway on December 1, 1924. Unfortunately five other plays also opened on Broadway on the same evening. Despite the competition *Close Harmony* got good reviews, mostly from Dorothy's critic friends, but in spite of a lot of publicity and paid advertising the play closed after only twenty-four performances. Although the collaboration with Elmer Rice had not led to much, she then collaborated with George Kaufman in writing the film script for *Business is Business*; the film was made by Paramount but was a flop.

The Roaring Twenties were in full swing, but to be one of the Bright Young Things required either lots and lots of money, celebrity, or talent. Broadway theaters were packed, Kaufman and Connelly enjoyed great success with their *Beggar on Horseback* at the Broadhurst theater, *The Other Rose* at the Morosco, Shaw's *St. Joan* at the Garrick, Laurence Eyre's comedy *The Merry Wives of Gotham* at the Henry Miller Theater, and *Laugh, Clown, Laugh* with Lionel Barrymore at the Belasco were playing to full and enthusiastic houses. Jazz bands and movies were competing with classical musicians such as Fritz Kreisler, Rachmaninoff, Jascha Heifetz, singer John McCormack, and Galli-Curci.

The jeweller George Glaenzer gave magnificent parties for celebrities and aristocrats including Lord Louis and Lady Edwina Mountbatten, Noël Coward, Douglas Fairbanks, Gertrude Lawrence, the Fred Astaires, Fanny Brice, George Gershwin, Maurice Chevalier, and Jascha Heifetz. Dorothy was ambivalent about the whole thing: she enjoyed her own celebrity and meeting some of the other celebrities, but disliked the heavy drinking, the noise, and the general indifference to the disparity between rich and poor and to social problems; her own socialist opinions she mostly kept to herself. She had, in spite of herself, become a pathological drinker, which magnified her depression. After a party, from which Benchley had accompanied her home to the Algonquin where she was staying, she made another suicide attempt with an overdose of barbiturates; she survived only because her absence from lunch the next day caused Benchley to become concerned, so he got a porter to open her room and he found her near death. Her hospitalization was brief, enlivened by gin which Heywood Broun fed her every evening. The suicide attempt was hushed up, and she was soon back again in the continuous party scene, both in New York and on Neshobe island or at Herbert Swope's house at Great Neck or his huge Manhattan apartment. New acquaintances included Ernest Hemingway, whose prose style she greatly admired for its clarity, brevity, and simplicity.

Donald Ogden Stewart was already working in Hollywood on a movie when Benchley decided to join him there, having been invited to be best man at Stewart's wedding to Beatrice Ames. Benchley's main achievement there was to break his leg; however, he did his bit as best man at the wedding in crutches, and also worked writing film scripts. But he didn't like Hollywood, which he described as "seventy-two suburbs in search of a city." Back at the Algonquin he found himself unable to work there on account of the proximity of the Round Table, so he moved to the Royalton Hotel which was nearby. However, a week later he was required back in Hollywood, and Dorothy took over his room to work in, writing for *The Bookman*, whose owner Seward Collins had commissioned her to write several articles. Her collection of verses *Enough Rope*, commissioned by Oppenheimer, appeared in print. It enjoyed enormous acclaim, sold out, and was reprinted thirteen times. Harold Ross wanted her to be literary critic of the *New Yorker*, an invitation she was happy to accept. The victims of her reviews must have been less so.

Her nom de plume was "Constant Reader," and her contributions appeared almost every week from October 1927 to May 1928. Many of them were flippant, sarcastic, and damning. Her review of Aimee Semple McPherson's autobiography was headed "Our Lady of the Loudspeaker," and described the author as "my favorite character in fiction." The heading for her review of *The Ideal System for Acquiring a Practical Knowledge of French* was "The Grandmother of the Aunt of the Gardener," and continued "how am I not to be bitter, who have stumbled solo about Europe, equipped only with 'Non, non et non!' and 'Ou est le lavabo des dames?'" An actor called Lou Tellegen wrote a book called *Women Have Been Kind*, for which the Constant Reader wrote: "Mr. Lou Tellegen has recently seen fit to write his memoirs. It is at least debatable that it would have been more public-spirited of him to have sent the results to the zoo." Mabel Dodge Luhan's *Background*, the first book in a planned series, elicited the comment: "It may be in her forthcoming volumes things will liven up a bit. But *Background* is to me as dull . . . as an album of old snapshots of somebody else's family group." Of Fannie Hurst's novel *A President Is Born* she wrote, "I have a deep admiration for Miss Hurst's work. Possibly in your company I must admit this with a coo of deprecating laughter as one confesses a fondness for comic-strips and chocolate almond bars—This, they say, is her Big Novel—I can find in it no character nor any thought to touch or excite me." An illustrated treatise for the general public by a doctor on the subject of appendicitis got the tongue-in-cheek praise, "For who that has stood bare-headed and beheld the peritoneum by moonlight can gaze unmoved by its likeness?"

Her first trip overseas was arranged by her friend Donald Ogden Stewart in the summer of 1926. She, Seward Collins, and Robert Benchley were to stay with Gerald and Sara Murphy at their villa at Cap d'Antibes. Also invited were Ernest Hemingway, Scott and Zelda Fitzgerald, Archibald MacLeish, and his wife Ada.

Time was spent enjoying the beaches and the Provence countryside, as well as gourmet dinners at good restaurants in Villefranche, Cannes (including the Carlton), Grasse, Mougins, Menton, and La Napoule. Scott and Zelda Fitzgerald seemed to spend most of their time fighting with one another. Celebrities abounded; writers included George Bernard Shaw, Somerset Maugham, who lived in his Villa Mauresque, and Ruth Gordon; there were actors such as Charlie Chaplin, Paulette Goddard, and Harpo Marx. Cole Porter, who also owned a villa in La Garoupe, gave lavish parties. Rudolf Valentino, Isadora Duncan, and Mistinguett were just a few of the other notables on the coast that summer. Elsa Maxwell, who was there, must have been in her element.

Dorothy Parker was becoming increasingly irritated with Seward Collins, with whom she'd been having an affair, and was once again drinking heavily. They were both in a small party invited by Hemingway to Spain, but although she idolized Hemingway she hated his preoccupation with bull-fighting, and was happy to accept an invitation from the Murphys to Paris, where Dorothy and Seward Collins were quarrelling furiously to the point where they separated, Collins returning alone to New York.

Parker resumed her work as literary reviewer for the *New Yorker* on her return from Europe. Of a play by A.A. Milne called *Give Me Yesterday* she wrote "If *Give Me Yesterday* is a fine play, I am Richard Brinsley Sheridan." She dismissed Katharine Hepburn's acting in a play with "Miss Hepburn ran the whole gamut of emotions from A to B." Her second book of verse, *Sunset Gun*, was now in print, repeating the success of *Enough Rope*.

However, she was not happy and was still drinking heavily. Benchley persuaded her to go to Alcoholics Anonymous, but she went only once. An operation for acute appendicitis seemed to have been a kind of mental tonic, for she resumed her party-going and her reviews for the *New Yorker*. Of an author she despised she wrote: "He's a writer for the ages. For the ages of four to eight." Her book of short stories, *Laments for the Living*, was printed, and she won a prize for the best American short story, but in spite of her growing income she was still on the edge of poverty. An ill-advised love affair ended badly, and she reacted with another suicide attempt by overdose, but recovered her characteristic bitchy sarcasm in a few weeks. She wrote of the play *House Beautiful* simply, "*House Beautiful* is the play lousy." A novel she did not like got "This is not a novel to be tossed aside lightly. It should be thrown with great force."

The stock market crash of 1929 did not affect her personally, for she had never invested in stocks, but her friend Herbert Swope lost an enormous sum and was in debt. She went to Hollywood on a contract with MGM purely to make some money, and like Benchley disliked California but did her work reliably until her contract was finished and she returned to New York.

In 1931 she was invited by the Murphys to their house in the Swiss Alps where she spent nearly a year. On her return to New York her new book of verses *Death and Taxes* came out, and she wrote the introduction to James Thurber's book of drawings *The Seal in the Bedroom*. The same year she met Alan Campbell, who had left a military academy to become an actor, and more or less fell in

love with her, though he was a bisexual. He moved
in with her, they became lovers and in 1934 were
married. He was, like her, half Jewish and half
Scottish, though on his father's side. He was
supremely efficient, did all the housework, the
cooking, kept the books, and looked after her
taxes, escorted her everywhere, and in time
became as much a member of the now diminished
"Vicious Circle" as she was.

In 1934 they moved to Hollywood at the suggestion of Leland Hayward who by then had
become Dorothy's and Alan's agent; he arranged a
contract for both of them with Paramount at $5,000
a week. They stayed at the Garden of Allah, a hotel
where Benchley, Noël Coward, and Ben Hecht
among others were living at the time. They wrote a
story for a film starring Carole Lombard, then
dialogue for two more films. Her initial dislike for
Hollywood lessened somewhat, principally on
account of the presence of numerous friends and
film stars who, like Bing Crosby and Helen Hayes,
became close friends. However, she generally
disliked writing for the screen, although Alan did,
and was good at it. They appeared in the credits of
numerous films and earned a lot of money.

After returning to New York from Hollywood
they decided to live in the country, in Bucks
County, Pennsylvania, where many of their friends
had houses. With their help, they found a big
house which they bought for $4,500, then spent
nearly $100,000 renovating it, including installing

a swimming pool. While living there Dorothy found she was pregnant, at the age of forty-three, but had a miscarriage. It was an event she seemingly pushed out of her mind, and never referred to again.

She returned to New York for a few days to get together with some old friends, then went back to the "farm" in Pennsylvania, but after a week was recalled to Hollywood by her agent Hayward to work for MGM on several films. She and Alan rented a splendid house in Beverly Hills, and wrote the final screenplay of *A Star Is Born*. This was nominated for an Oscar but did not win. They worked on other films, some good, some bad, but again Dorothy was distressed at the work she had to do. She did, however, join enthusiastically in the social round; at one of her parties in Beverly Hills the guests included Robert Sherwood, by now a Pulitzer Prize-winning playwright, Robert Benchley, and F. Scott Fitzgerald.

She was, however, becoming more politically aware and involved, with a definite bias towards socialism and indeed communism. Although she wrote a few pieces for the *New Yorker*, most of her work was for Hollywood. Her office at MGM was alongside those of Somerset Maugham, Thornton Wilder, William and Sinclair Lewis. Aldous Huxley and Christopher Isherwood were also in Hollywood at that time (1937).

Her most faithful ally in her political work was Donald Ogden Stewart, who was now a successful writer of screenplays, satires, and novels. They organized fund-raising events for radical causes, among which were those involved with minorities and the poor in the United States, and in particular with the Republicans in the Spanish Civil War. They had been instrumental in the formation of the Hollywood Anti-Nazi League in 1936. Dorothy Parker, Dashiell Hammett, and Lillian Hellman were the organizers of the Screen Writers' Guild.

Alan Campbell was not keen on this type of activity. He and Dorothy were weekend guests at William Randolph Hearst's castle at San Simeon, and returned from time to time to their country place; however, their relationship apart from work was beginning to deteriorate. Nonetheless they went together to Paris, where they met the Murphys and James Thurber again. But Dorothy's main interest in Europe at that time was Spain, so she left her Paris friends and her husband to report on the Civil War there. In Madrid she met Hemingway, who was there for the same purpose, endured an air-raid in Valencia, then returned to Paris. There she wrote a story about the plight of the poor in Spain, and sent it to Harold Ross at the *New Yorker* who published it. She briefly became a Roman Catholic, but abandoned that church when Madrid was taken by Franco's troops. The fact that the Catholic Church in Spain supported Franco became too much for her to take.

She continued to be active in left-wing organizations and causes, which Alan deplored because he felt, rightly, that Hollywood producers in 1939 were reluctant to employ writers who had a pro-communist reputation. The war began with Germany and Russia carving up Poland; Dorothy was totally disillusioned and resigned from all her left-wing committees, devoting herself only to writing. Her fifth book *Here Lies* was published, she wrote a few pieces for magazines and assisted Lillian Hellman in writing the screen version of Hellman's play *The Little Foxes*. However, in 1941 she and Alan resumed writing for the movies. In December 1941 the Japanese attacked the American fleet at Pearl Harbor. Alan enlisted in the army, and after training was sent overseas. Dorothy tried to join the Women's Army Corps, but was turned down, possibly because of her previous political affiliations, then tried to be accredited as an over-seas war correspondent, but was denied this for the same reason. She continued writing, moving around between New York, Hollywood, and the farm at West End, and associating with her friends Lillian Hellman and Beatrice Ames, the ex-wife of Donald Ogden Stewart.

Alan was now in London enjoying himself. He was leading an active life, involved with people such as Laurence Olivier, George Kaufman, Binkie Beaumont, the Lunts; he wrote to Dorothy who was becoming jealous, and wrote him angry letters. Soon he stopped writing altogether, so then did she. She was still fond of him, and was bitterly disappointed when he was not demobilized but required to remain in London. She was drinking excessively, and informed him in 1945 that she was going to file for divorce, but delayed doing so until 1947, when she obtained a divorce in Las Vegas, and sold the farm at a substantial loss.

She collaborated with a writer called Ross Evans on a film script of Oscar Wilde's *Lady Windermere's Fan*, and subsequently on a play based on Charles Lamb's relationship with his sister Mary. The play opened in Dallas where it did well, but it failed to be produced in New York, or London, or even at the Edinburgh Festival. She and Evans became lovers, she spent a lot of money on him but the affair did not survive a holiday in Mexico, where he was crude and abusive and sent her back to New York.

Dorothy and Lillian Hellman were both unwilling witnesses before Senator McCarthy's Un-American Activities committee, on account of their being both Hollywood personalities and affiliated with a variety of left-wing organizations, but the case against both of them was dropped.

In the 1950s Dorothy stayed at the Volney Hotel in New York, since she could no longer afford to stay at the Plaza. Alan phoned her from Hollywood; he was living at Norma Place and invited her to join him there. She did, and soon they decided to re-marry; the renewed marriage was turbulent, they were both drinking and quarrelling incessantly, and were unemployed to the point of having to apply for unemployment compensation.

She did, however, write a play with her old friend the playwright Arnold d'Usseau, based on her experiences at the Volney Hotel, called *Ladies of the Corridor*. It opened in New York in October 1953 but ran for only forty-five performances. In 1955 the *New Yorker* accepted two of her stories, and she was persuaded to write also for *Esquire*, which she occasionally did. One way or another she and Alan managed to survive.

Alan died in June 1963, aged fifty-eight, of a possibly accidental overdose of barbiturates and alcohol; Dorothy was now seventy and in spite of her celebrity was more and more alone. However, Wyatt Cooper and his wife Gloria Vanderbilt arranged a magnificent party for her, having had a gorgeous gown made for her to wear at it.

Three months later, on June 7, 1967, Dorothy Parker died in her room at the Volney Hotel, alone. She was not quite seventy-four years of age.

8

Restaurant Row and the Fringe Theaters of New York

Restaurant Row is found on West 44th Street, where all the restaurants serve pre-theater dinners. Famous eating establishments jostle against the less renowned. Joe Allen's and Barbetta's are the most famous, but if you want less expensive food just walk down two blocks to West 42nd Street where most of the fringe or off-Broadway theaters are to be found. This is called Theater Row. There are many restaurants which cater to the off-Broadway audiences.

Joe Allen has restaurants in New York, London, Paris, Miami, and Maine (in the summer). The one in New York is the original and on the walls there are the usual theater posters except, Joe said with a smile, the plays were all flops on Broadway! He owns Orso's next door and the one in London. He says that he is semi-retired now with a house in Italy, but it is hard to believe.

Off-Broadway producers present plays by unknown playwrights, often without name players, and many of them are subsequently transferred to

Broadway. They are the equivalent of the fringe theaters in London, although often larger, and a literary feast can be found in new material and a buffet of new plays often featuring young performers who are just beginning their careers. It is similar to going into a newly opened restaurant before it has been reviewed. Here are the names of some of the best-known theaters, but there are many more, although some of them don't stay open on a year-round basis.

Circle in the Square is New York's oldest company, founded in 1951. Theodore Mann produced many of O'Neill's plays there. Jim Dale worked there in 1974 in *Scapino*, Rex Harrison in *Heartbreak House* in 1983, and Tom Courtenay in *Uncle Vanya* in 1995. Many of the productions transferred to Broadway, and numerous awards include Tonys, Obies, and Drama Desk Awards. Off-Broadway theaters first produced plays such as Beckett's *Endgame*, Joe Orton's *What the Butler Saw*, *The Elephant Man*, Caryl Churchill's *Cloud Nine*, and Alan Bennett's *A Chorus Line*.

The Manhattan Theater Club on West 55th Street started in 1970 to develop new work. Lynne Meadow, the Artistic Director since 1972, says that their aim is to present well-crafted, challenging plays by major writers from the U.S. and around the world. Known as the MTC to New Yorkers, Lynne received the 1989 Drama Desk Award for setting such high standards at MTC and encouragng new playwrights as well as importing plays from abroad.

Joseph Papp (1921–91) was founder of the New York Shakespeare Festival in 1954. He began his career as a stage manager on Broadway, but then in 1966 obtained a huge hundred-year-old building at 425 Lafayette Street, on New York's Lower East Side, and there began the Shakespeare Theatre Workshop. There are five theater spaces within the building, and in 1992 the huge complex was named after Papp, whose influence in the theater will long be remembered. There are numerous cafés on Lafayette Street where the prices are reasonable and where the actors eat.

Broadway reaches up to the Lincoln Center and there are two theaters within the building which also houses the Opera House. They are the Mitzi E. Newhouse and Vivian Beaumont Theaters. There is a row of restaurants on Broadway opposite the Lincoln Center and most of them feature outdoor dining, where patrons can sit and view the passing parade. Fiorello's is one of the best known and many celebrities including Placido Domingo, Kevin Kline, and Sian Phillips dine there before or after the theater. They serve mostly Italian cuisine and there is a delicious seafood buffet as well. These restaurants are very busy during the summer months, with brunch being the most popular time. On Sundays most of the restaurants in this area feature a 'Special Brunch' which usually includes a complimentary glass of champagne, a bloody mary, or wine. Brunch usually extends until about 4 p.m.

One of the most celebrated off-Broadway theaters is the Lucille Lortel Theater on Christopher Street, named after one of the best-known women in New York theater. She began producing plays in 1941 in her barn in Westport, Connecticut, and it became a great showcase for new plays during the summer season. She remodelled it and called it the White Barn Theater. In 1955 she acquired the Theatre de Lys in New York, and it was renamed the Lortel in 1981. It served as a transfer theater for the more successful plays at the White Barn. Caryl Churchill's *Cloud Nine* was first produced here following plays by Bertolt Brecht, Jean Genet, Athol Fugard, and Eugene Ionesco. Her first production in New York was *The Threepenny Opera*, which ran for seven years. She is a co-founder of the American Shakespeare Festival, and a documentary film was made about her, titled *The Queen of Off Broadway*.

Off-Broadway theater actors have included Kevin Kline (*Hamlet*), Geraldine Fitzgerald (*Mass Appeal*), George C. Scott (*Present Laughter* and *Design for Living*), also Julie Harris, Claire Bloom, Meryl Streep, Stacy Keach, and Jason Robards Jr. Off-Broadway is a place for well-known actors to try unfamiliar roles. In 1955 the *Village Voice* newspaper established the Obie Awards to reward off-Broadway productions, and the Lucille Lortel awards are also given each year.

The Cherry Lane Theater on picturesque Commerce Street has a small pub near the theater

where actors and patrons mix after the performance. The actress Kim Hunter lived above the
theater until her death in 2002. Her kitchen was
directly above the stage and she used to say that
when she went to bed at night she hoped the
current play downstairs did not have any gunshots
or thunder in the plot, or anyone cooking on stage.

Lynn Redgrave has starred in many Broadway
productions; however, in 2003 she went to the off-
Broadway Minetta Lane Theater, to star in Alan
Bennett's new collection of monologues, and after
the show we found two Italian restaurants side by
side within a short distance.

Finally, the show *Forbidden Broadway* is worth
noting but keeps changing its location, so check
the newspaper listings. This show is a revue,
well worth a visit if you enjoy watching
American actors lampooning British shows as
well as all the current Broadway hits. Over
drinks and food you can watch wicked imperson-
ations of Julie Andrews, Andrew Lloyd Webber,
and Natasha Richardson, which are all part of the
game. This revue updates its material each
season to parody the current Broadway shows.
Created by Gerard Alessandrini, who is a genius
in writing new lyrics to Broadway songs, it has
been running since 1982. After Madonna had
made her Broadway debut, Alessandrini changed
the lyrics of the famous song in *My Fair Lady,*
"The rain in Spain stays mainly in the plain," to
"We tried in vain to train Madonna's brain."

Off off-Broadway became established in the early 1960s. There are now around 200 theater spaces in Manhattan, tiny theater stages in old churches, lofts, cafés, and sometimes store fronts. These productions can range from traditional three-act plays to one-man shows. Again it is necessary to check each theater's program on a weekly basis, as many of them have short runs, or a repertory system with different plays on alternate evenings.

In 1975 when Robert Mosher, director of Playwright Horizons, needed a theater, he discovered a group of buildings on West 42nd Street which were being used as massage parlors, porno shops, and so on. He rented one space and ended up by completely transforming the area. Then he successfully obtained an alternative theater district a few blocks west of Broadway for Off-Off-Broadway companies. The 42nd Street Redevelopment Corporation was formed, and they bought the whole block of buildings. In 1978, with much publicity, Theater Row was officially opened. There were ten companies, all operating on a non-profit basis, and some of these companies have since been upgraded to Off-Broadway status.

Restaurants and small cafés opened, and there is a subsidized housing complex for actors called the Manhattan Plaza nearby. Theater Row now houses the following theaters: the Acting Company, Alice's Fourth Floor, Theatre Arielle, the Samuel Beckett, the Harold Clurman, the Douglas Fairbanks, the George S. Kaufman, INTAR Hispanic American Arts Center, the John Houseman Center, the Judith

Anderson, the Nat Horne Musical Theater, Playwrights Horizons (main stage and studio theaters), and the Theater Row theater. Many British actors have performed there, including Fiona Shaw in T.S. Eliot's *The Wasteland*.

A word must be recorded here about the Theater Guild, which was formed in 1915 by a group of young actors and writers who were dissatisfied with the commercial theater of their day. They organized a company called the Washington Square Players—way off-Broadway—and they were ambitious enough to try to become a professional company which would eventually present plays on Broadway. The Guild's record is unique in the history of American theater, and it is only recently that it has ceased production.

Café Cino was the first Off-Off-Broadway theater, where Joe Cino presented plays in his coffee-house in 1959. Café La Ma Ma was founded by Ellen Stewart in 1962, and Theater Genesis by Ralph Cook in 1964. New playwrights were discovered including Sam Shepard, Terence McNally, and Lanford Wilson.

"Food for Thought" is a lunchtime series of readings by celebrity actors at the National Arts Club in Gramercy Park reading portions of new plays and discussing them with the playwrights. It has been very successful and is the first time theater has been presented at lunchtime in New York. Many of the actors enjoy participating even if they are playing on Broadway in the evenings.

9

Ivor Novello's Favorites

At first sight there does not seem to be much of a link between Ivor Novello and New York. He died, aged fifty-eight, in 1951, so he didn't have the same opportunities for television appearances as his friend and friendly rival, Noël Coward. Noël was able to redefine his public image in the 1950s through East Coast television specials and through regular and highly paid cabaret appearances in Las Vegas. Ivor had achieved considerable success in London during and immediately after the First World War through a string of late-night revues at fashionable theaters, and his facility for a catchy tune would have ensured U.S. success had he lived long enough to follow Noël's example.

One of Ivor's favorite places to go in New York was Peacock Alley at the Waldorf Astoria for champagne cocktails and to view the beautiful murals which can still be seen there today. This of course was after Prohibition, and the jazz age of the 1920s. He represented the quintessential Englishman with his impeccable wardrobe and manners. The Rainbow Room at Rockefeller Plaza

was another favorite and since its recent renova-
tion it now looks as it did in the 1930s, with the
Art Deco features fully restored. The fashionable
thing to do in those days was to appear there after
the theater and people still dance today on the
original revolving dance floor. (See "Famous
Theatrical Restaurants.")

Floor shows were presented with a full orchestra
and stars like Bea Lillie would descend the long
curved staircase above the orchestra on stage.
Cabaret stars loved the room because they could
make such dramatic entrances. The view from the
room is spectacular, overlooking all the lights of
Manhattan at night for miles around.

This was the era of prawn cocktails and steak
Diane, when the waiters would cook at your table
and the special desserts were Bombe Alaska or
Crepe Suzettes. Flames were kept alive by brandy
and liquers as the waiter would perform beside you
with deft movements to get the food from the fire
on to your plate. The cabaret shows were inspired
by those of Novello's old friend Marlene Dietrich.

Ivor Novello is primarily known for his
musicals, which made him the most popular and
prolific composer of British musicals until
Andrew (now Lord) Lloyd Webber began his
meteoric rise to fame in the 1970s. Ivor's shows are
generally described as "Ruritanian" and are, in a
sense, operettas, drawing on the great romantic
tradition (and the often overlooked comedy) of the
Viennese masters like Franz Lehar, whose greatest

work, *The Merry Widow*, was seen by the young Ivor Novello twenty-seven times!

These musicals of Ivor's, which earned him a fortune in England (he had a London penthouse, a country mansion, and a house in Jamaica, a Rolls-Royce, and numerous servants, as well as an army of secretaries, helpers, and awe-struck camp followers), never transferred to Broadway.

New York first made an impact on him as a teenager, when he traveled to North America with his mother, Clara Novello Davies. This formidable woman was small, round, and with a fiery Welsh temperament and a talent that was propelled—and sometimes damaged—by her enormous determination to succeed. This talent was passed on to her son, who displayed it in a far less blatant manner, and as soon as she was able to assure herself that her only child was indeed the musical prodigy that she had prayed for, she groomed him to be a great composer.

Even when Ivor was at the top of his profession, a film star, playwright, actor, and composer of smash hit musicals, she insisted on carrying on with her own career as a choir-mistress and singing teacher. It was in the first capacity that she took Ivor to the States in 1911, where he caught the New World love of modernity that was also to win over the young Prince of Wales, later Edward VIII.

It was in the second capacity that she took a studio in New York for six months of the year, having been as impressed by the size, splendor, and vitality of New York as her impressionable and theater-mad son. Clara Novello Davies was not a woman to let anything as inartistic as a war get in the way, so even when the German U-boats (that were to sink the *Lusitania* and bring the United States, reluctantly, into World War I) threatened civilian shipping in the Atlantic sea-lanes, she insisted on crossing the "pond" to bring her unique and highly effective singing and breath-control methods to a willing, well-off clientèle of New York ladies.

By and large Clara fitted into New York society very well, though her deliberate flouting of conventions by inviting blacks (albeit statuesque and talented ones who would have been an adornment to any event) to her lavish parties did not go down terribly well with many of her neighbors. Party-giving was in her blood, so the money she made from her fashionable lessons was always eaten up by the time her "season" ended, so she was compelled, for financial reasons as much as artistic or career ones, to return each following year.

If Ivor Novello's first experience of New York was as a good-looking appendage to his mother's entourage, his next extended visit was as a strikingly handsome film star and successful actor and playwright—in short, a star. Having become rich and famous at the age of twenty-one, in 1914, by composing the extraordinarily poignant and popular anthem to a lost generation of war-embittered soldiers, "Keep the Home Fires Burning," he went on to write music for revues, and then, in 1919, the year after the war finally dragged to a close (before beginning a re-run, in 1939) he became a movie star.

Louis Mercanton, the French film director, spotted Ivor's photo in an agent's file, and although he was there as a composer, his Italianate dark good looks and the soon-to-be-famous profile clinched the deal for Mercanton, who cast him as the lead in *L'Appel du Sang*, a torrid melodrama about a young man who falls in love with a Sicilian girl and is murdered by a jealous relative.

This early success was followed up with *The White Rose*, directed by the great D.W. Griffith, who was already past his creative prime, but still a name to reckon with. The story goes that Griffith, when in London, used to dine at the Savoy, one of London's most prestigious and exclusive restaurants (as Paul Robeson was to find—he was allowed to appear on stage in *Othello* at the neighboring Savoy Theatre, but not permitted to dine at the hotel). Ivor, knowing that the great man was in town and looking for a leading man for his next film, made sure he had a table near the director's, and made equally sure that Griffith caught the full force of his devastating good looks, especially the Novello profile. As Noël Coward was later to quip, "There are two perfect things in this world—my brain and Ivor's profile."

Having succeeded in catching D.W. Griffith's attention, Novello was cast in *The White Rose*, and went on from there to star in a variety of British silent movies, including Alfred Hitchcock's first success, *The Lodger* (1926). He combined this film career with the life of an actor and playwright (which ensured he got the lead roles that suited him most), and so, when he arrived by liner at New York in 1930, the American public was used to seeing photos and reading gossip about him in film magazines and the popular press.

Interest in the British visitor, who came to Broadway to appear in *Symphony in Two Flats*, a play that was equally divided between comedy and tragedy, was heightened by the fact that Ivor was rumored to be in love with fellow passenger, Gladys Cooper (grandmother of the theater historian, critic, and *Playbill* writer, Sheridan Morley). Ivor and Gladys were indeed very close, and had co-starred in a silent movie about the life of Bonnie Prince Charlie (1923), but both their hearts were otherwise engaged, and they were, to use the classic phrase, just good friends.

The summer of 1930 was not the ideal time to arrive on Broadway with a foreign play. Quite apart from the seasonal warm weather, which in pre-air-conditioning days made play-going an uncomfortable business (as American visitors to London still find all too often!), *Symphony in Two Flats* was not Ivor's most brilliant play. The other factor in this commercial equation was that the Wall Street Crash of Fall 1929 was less than a year earlier, and the financial repercussions were still being felt by a great many people. Regular theater-goers were an endangered species.

The play was put on by that great theater dynasty, the Shuberts, and taken off again soon after. Ivor's determination to succeed, nurtured by his mother and reinforced by a decade of stardom, meant that he was not about to turn tail and head back for London. Although his mother's glory days as the diva teacher of New York were now over, it was inconceivable to him to be defeated by a city he admired and loved, and which his mother had, in her own way, conquered. He appealed to the Shuberts to try with a more commercial play of his, and they had the good sense to agree.

The Truth Game was staged at the Ethel Barrymore Theater, and co-starred Billie Burke, the wife of the legendary showman, Florenz Ziegfeld, who threw a huge party for Novello at his Hudson River home. Given this combination of acting talent, and the strength of the play's script, it is not surprising that the show was a hit with critics and public alike. During the run of *The Truth Game* Ivor became very friendly with a wealthy young American, Richard Rose, who was later to co-produce several of his shows in England. It was Rose who found Ivor a new flat after Bea Lillie, in whose home Ivor had originally stayed, returned to New York from London.

Elsa Maxwell was giving her parties both in New York and London, and Ivor was always invited as they had known each other since she first became successful as a hostess. She was lavish with her food, providing pounds of smoked salmon and shrimp, huge roasts of beef carved into small pieces to be eaten off the buffet table with tiny roast potatoes, and mounds of strawberries and cream as well as all the most expensive ice creams she could find.

Ivor knew how to concoct a bath full of gin (this was of course during Prohibition) so the party clearly went with a swing and Ivor's life-long ability to attract the brightest lights in the theater and film world meant that the first-night party was described as "The Party of the Stars."

It was this prolonged experience of New York, together with his more general admiration for American talent, that led to Ivor's habit of casting American leading ladies in his very British (or, at least, given the operetta background, European) musicals. Before discussing them it might be helpful just to list the best of them: *Glamorous Night* and *King's Rhapsody* could really be described as Ruritanian, in the sense of being set in make-believe European kingdoms. *The Dancing Years* was set in Vienna, over a period of some twenty-five years. If shanty towns and palm-fringed isles seem ridiculously romantic and escapist, it must not be forgotten that Ivor's shows also included very modern settings—such as the beauty salon frequented by society ladies in *Careless Rapture*, and the bustling fairground scene set on London's Hampstead Heath in the same musical. The liner in *Glamorous Night* represented the latest in the travel chic that led to a golden age of Art Deco floating palaces between the two world wars.

It was on such a liner that Novello traveled to New York as a young man, and the harbor on the Hudson would have been a familiar sight to him, as would the restaurants, particularly Sardi's, shops and hotels of Manhattan. He was not fond of being pestered in the street, which is why he preferred to travel everywhere, however short the distance (including just around the corner from the Theatre Royal, Drury Lane, to his flat in the Aldwych), in his enormous Rolls-Royce.

This desire to preserve his distance from the fans when off duty extended to hotels. When holidaying in England (which was fairly rare, as he preferred to escape to the sun—hence his home in Jamaica) he would sometimes stay in a small, family-run hotel rather than somewhere grand, but pay for all the rooms at once, ensuring that the place was packed with friends, thus keeping out unwanted attention from strangers. He made an exception in New York, however, for if he couldn't stay at a friend's flat then he stayed at the Algonquin, enjoying its style and artistic atmosphere.

One of Novello's last holidays was in the winter of 1950/51, when he went to Jamaica via New York, in order to get some much needed rest and sunshine. His last great hit, *King's Rhapsody*, had been playing to packed houses at the Palace Theatre (where *Les Miserables* has been running since 1984) and he wanted a break—not least because he had also been working on his final show (written for Cicely Courtneidge, and in which he didn't appear), called *Gay's the Word*.

Shortly after *Gay's the Word* opened at the Saville Theatre in upper Shaftesbury Avenue (it is now a cinema) Ivor gave his last performance in *King's Rhapsody*, on the evening of March 5, 1951. After the show he was driven in the Rolls back to the flat, where he met Tom Arnold, the producer of most of his shows. They had the inevitable bottle of champagne and discussed show business matters and theatrical gossip—both subjects dear to Ivor's heart.

That heart, which was universally acknowledged to be the most generous in the British theater, finally beat its last after a heart attack in the early hours of March 6. His friends, Bobby Andrews and Olive Gilbert, who appeared with him in many shows, and who were pillars of his private as well as professional life, were with him. They called a doctor, but he could do nothing.

Ivor's death marked the immediate end of his theatrical empire, and his passing marked the passing, too, of a whole musical tradition. London was almost immediately conquered by the new, postwar American musical, which Ivor had loved, learned from, but resisted—and resisted successfully: *King's Rhapsody* had taken the biggest box office advance in West End history, and more than held its own against *Oklahoma*.

The irony is that this composer, now seen as old-fashioned and peculiarly English in style and appeal, had been so enthused, from his teens onwards, by the energy and excitement of the New York theater scene, and had imported some of the best examples of American stage technique in order to create and maintain his own highly distinctive series of musicals. Therefore, although Ivor Novello was a unique writer, composer, and performer, he in some ways symbolizes the way that Broadway and the West End have, over the years, and, despite being set up as rivals by commentators on both sides of the Atlantic, enjoyed a mutually beneficial and creative relationship. This has served to enrich both theatrical cultures, and, despite their real and important differences, it has brought them together. It may be a long-distance relationship but it's a relationship all the same, and one that continues to flourish, to the benefit of both the West End and Broadway.

10

Following in Noël Coward's Footsteps

After Noël Coward found success in New York, he was wined and dined by celebrities everywhere. In his diaries you can read all about the places where he had lunch or dinner. Quite often he describes what he ate and who he was with. For example, on one of his visits to New York in 1947, on the day of his arrival by ship, he lunched at the Colony with friends, went on to have mint juleps with Ina Claire and her husband at 2 p.m., then dinner with Jack Wilson before seeing a performance of *Brigadoon* at the Ziegfeld Theater. He finished up at the Stork Club with Dorothy Parker.

However, before his success, during his first two visits to New York he had to rely on the hospitality of friends, as he couldn't afford to eat at restaurants. Laurette Taylor, who was starring on Broadway, befriended Coward and in 1922 she and her family moved into 50 Riverside Drive. That winter she played host to the world of American theater, taking in actors and directors. A young Noël Coward was among them. The sound of the piano bewitched into melody meant that Noël was in the living room whiling away an hour or so until someone came home. Each family member in turn would stop on the way upstairs, lean over the balcony and invite him to stay for dinner. "Thank you darling, I'd love to," Noël would reply, smiling up at each. The family were very kind, generous, and eccentric. Every Sunday Laurette gave a dinner party, when the family would instigate complicated and intricate party games. Noël Coward wrote, "It was inevitable that someone should eventually utilize portions in a play, and I'm only grateful to Fate that no guest thought of writing *Hay Fever* before I did." Marguerite Courtney (Laurette Taylor's daughter) wrote that later, when word drifted across the Atlantic that Coward's new play *Hay Fever* was supposed to be an intimate picture of the family, Laurette was hurt. After seeing the play in New York, she found it hard to forgive him, and the group of rugged individualists whom he depicted were not her family at all.

Another larger than life Englishman who was in New York at the time, and whom Coward met, was Ronald Colman. He was soon to have the most famous little moustache since Charlie Chaplin, but at the time was as much a penniless hopeful as Coward himself. Noël got over the lack of money as he did all obstacles—with charm and determination. Accounts of his time in New York alternate between accounts of poverty (having to borrow money from Lynn Fontanne, for example) and descriptions of society parties on the Upper East Side, and country house parties. When he left for England, as the leaves began to fall in Central Park, Noël Coward had failed to make the professional breakthrough that he had anticipated, but had launched himself on the social scene, and was confident, and determined, that he would return.

If any one Englishman can be said to sum up the English affair with New York, it must surely be Sir Noël Coward. In many ways a "typical" Englishman of a certain class, but with a style, talent, and mode of speech that made him a twentieth-century icon and very much a one-off, Coward has been described as the first pop star. This description may seem very much at odds with his elegant, suave image, but his very modern awareness of the importance of image cultivation and self-publicity mark him out as one of the avant garde in terms of popular entertainment.

Noël Coward's reputation is as a member of the upper class—albeit with a theatrical bent rather than the traditional interests of hunting, shooting, and fishing. In fact, he was the son of poorly-off parents, who through a positively American strength of will and ambition (helped a little, of course, by an enormous talent as a wit, playwright, screenwriter, composer, and singer) re-invented himself and became one of the world's first and most enduring superstars: rich, famous, friend of royalty. No wonder he was nicknamed the Master.

While trying to break into Broadway, Noël met two vitally important friends, Alfred Lunt and Lynn Fontanne. They were living at Dr. Round's boardinghouse on 130 West 70th Street. Dr. Round was a remarkable woman who ran a welcoming house that opened its doors to actors, however poor. The building still stands and was the scene of what Coward said were prophetic orgies, and he visited there frequently. He wrote and co-starred in *Design for Living* some years later, when he and the Lunts were safely successful. The play has been sporadically revived since the 1930s, but is primarily of interest for its biographical background rather than its artistic merit. The three of them became life-long friends, and Coward often visited and stayed in their country home, Ten Chimneys, which has just been opened to the public.

While the acting work was in abeyance, Noël wrote stories which he was able to sell, including to *Vanity Fair*. This provided him with periodic bursts of income, but he had to cut his cloth according to his means, so instead of the lavish lunches that he was so greatly to enjoy once he became a success, he dined, in less than splendor, at an Italian deli in McDougal Street.

When eating at home, bereft of air conditioning and in the full blast of a New York summer, he prepared his food stark naked, unaware that his anatomy was easily viewed by passers-by and neighbors. In one of those famous incidents that swiftly became part of Noël Coward folklore, he was called upon by a bad-tempered policeman, whose indignation was quickly overcome—despite his obvious disadvantage—by Noël's extraordinary charm. Aided, one suspects, by the fact that the charm was accompanied by half a bottle of wine, the policeman not only left Noël to his own devices, but gave him his revolver, as the neighborhood was notoriously dangerous. It makes a great story, but one can't help thinking that the likelihood of a hardened precinct cop handing over his revolver to a strange, naked Englishman, let alone leaving it at his apartment, beggars belief. Mind you, quite a lot of Coward's career was distinctly larger than life . . .

The fact that he did return, throughout his career, was evidence of the two-way love affair between Coward and New York. On his second visit, in 1924, his songs were performed in André Charlot's *Revue of 1924*—a show that may not have had a very exciting title (apart from a starry cast that included Jack Buchanan and Gertrude Lawrence), but caught the mood of the age and became a hit. It is easy, at this distance, to forget that memories of World War I were still very much in people's minds.

The hedonism of the 1920s was a reaction to the horrors of the war and this was a period when the well-to-do had the resources to live well and dine late. Revues were the perfect entertainment for smart New York (and London) society—clever and amusing yet easily digestible. Pictures taken at the time show the audiences to be beautifully and formally dressed, determined to have a glamorous night out. They would have been astonished had they seen the dressing down that generally takes place today, particularly in London.

As a young man Coward was inspired, as were so many of his generation, by the excitement and vitality of America in general. "I Like America" was in many ways an anthem to this period of his life, New York in particular, and in middle age he was to find America a refuge and a source of income—the New World coming to the rescue of the Old.

It is easy to forget how, in the 1920s, when Noël Coward began to achieve the fame and fortune that his mother had been so sure was his birthright, America seemed to be a heady mixture of the safe (no ghastly tropical diseases like the profitable but perilous parts of the British Empire that had earned nicknames like "The White Man's Grave") and the exciting. It was a Brave New World that combined democracy with capitalism, that welcomed the huddled masses, yearning to be free, but which exported jazz, affordable motor cars, and a breezy, fresh attitude to life that stood in stark contrast to the shattered societies of a Europe that had been broken by World War I.

In England, even the Prince of Wales, the inheritor of Empire, the future King and Emperor, took American fashions to heart, and adopted—in rebellion against his father—a half-cockney, half-

Above: Alexander Cohen, the Broadway producer who brought dozens of British productions to Broadway, seen here with John Gielgud and Vivien Leigh. (© *Bettmann/ CORBIS*)

Right: Liza Minnelli with Jean-Pierre Aumont, the French singer, after she opened at the Empire Room of the Waldorf Astoria. (*CORBIS*)

Mrs. Robert Lanz and Elizabeth Sharland talk to Yul Brynner at the Hard Rock Café after the opening night of *The King and I* on Broadway in 1983. (*Author*)

George Lang, the owner, outside Café des Artistes. The restaurant features famous murals of naked nymphs by artist Christy Chandler. Customers include Placido Domingo, Luciano Pavarotti, and stars of the Metropolitan Opera located nearby. (*Author*)

The interior of Sardi's, one of New York's most famous theater restaurants, well known for hosting Broadway first-night parties. (*Author*)

Rock Hudson (left), Gregory Peck (right), and Douglas Fairbanks Jr. at the opening party for *Sweeney Todd* at Sardi's. (© *Bettmann/CORBIS*)

Left: Exterior of the Algonquin Hotel, New York, which many British actors make their home from home. *(© CORBIS)*

Below: Barrie Ingham, Rosemary Harris, and Judy Campbell at the Round Table at the Algonquin celebrating after a performance of the author's *From Shakespeare to Coward*. (*Author*)

Above: Alfred Lunt and Lynn Fontanne with Noel Coward at Ten Chimneys. Coward had his own room in the Lunts' house, which is now open to the public. (*Warren O'Brien Family Collection at SHSW. © Ten Chimneys*)

Right: The St. Regis Hotel. The Oliviers stayed here during their first New York visit. (*Author*)

The exterior of the Plaza Hotel showing the Oyster Bar, which is very popular at the cocktail hour. (*Author*)

The bar in the Rainbow Room situated at the top of the Rockefeller Center. The room features a revolving dance floor and a terrific view of New York City. (© *Bob Krist/CORBIS*)

Right: The exterior of the Lambs Club, when it was situated at 128 West 44th Street. One of the oldest private theater clubs in Manhattan, it later moved to West 51st Street. (© *Underwood & Underwood/ CORBIS*)

Below: Robert de Niro, Whoopi Goldberg, and Ted Danson at the Friars Club. (© *Mitchell Gerber/CORBIS*)

Above: Joe Allen outside his restaurant in New York. He owns several others on both sides of the Atlantic, including London and Paris. (*Author*)

Left: The Actors' Church, showing the charming lych-gate at the entrance to the church and the quiet close, where often on a sunny day people come from nearby office buildings to eat their lunch. (*Author*)

American accent that was a radical departure from the usual tones of upper-class England.

It was not surprising, therefore, that the young Noël Coward decided that he would travel to New York, hoping that he would take the city by storm. His thoughts seemed to be on the lines of the song made famous by Frank Sinatra. If Coward could make it there, people back in London would have to sit up and take notice. He would, literally, have arrived. It was with the glamorous image of New York in his mind, and with his name in lights on Broadway as his most heartfelt wish, that Coward had traveled, on a Cunard liner (naturally!), across the Atlantic, accompanied by an aristocratic English friend, Jeffrey Amherst, in May 1921.

The *Aquitania* seemed to symbolize the glamorous world that Coward was convinced was his by right, but fate gave him a warning of the trials ahead when many of the ship's crew, including, vitally, the cooks, went on strike! Having survived this example of backstage rebellion, Coward caught his first glimpse of Manhattan on a gorgeous June morning.

Even today, the experience of gliding past the skyscrapers and docks of New York is exciting, however often one may have done it, but to a young man in the early 1920s it must have been breathtaking. Coward recalled his first impression in 1921:

There will always be a stinging enchantment in this arrival. Even now, when I know it so well in every aspect, my heart jumps a little. Then it was entirely new to me. We slid gently past Battery Park, still green with early summer. The skyscrapers moved gracefully aside to show still further vistas, and, a long way below us, platoons of straw hats passed by on ferry boats. As we drew near the dock, several fussy little tugs came out to meet us and finally, after tremendous efforts, succeeded in coaxing and nuzzling us alongside.

A stickler for doing things well, and aiming for the best, Coward made straight for the Algonquin Hotel, but he could barely wait to deliver his suitcases before rushing off to Broadway. For Noël had theater in the blood: not for nothing was this the author of "The Boy Actor," a superb and moving poem about a child actor whose formative years were spent, not on the games field, but on stage. Not for him the cheers of his fellows as he scored a goal—his adrenaline surged not to muddy fields but to the smell of greasepaint, the tattered glamor of theater dressing rooms, the sound of the front-of-house orchestra, the thrill of an extra curtain call.

Coward's delight in Broadway reflects the fact that, for all the British pride in London's theaterland, even the most patriotic of British actors (and Noël Coward, after all, wrote that love song to the city, "London Pride," at the height of World War II) realized that Broadway was somewhere special.

Not just because of the traditions of its stately theaters (many of which were as old as anything London had to offer, after all), but because of the sheer electricity in the air (and on the billboards!), the use of the latest marketing techniques to make the desirable seem unmissable.

The excitement that was a hallmark of Broadway was also reflected in the hectic social life of the city, particularly among the rather more adventurous theatrical set. Coward made many new friends as well as bumping into chums from London who, like him, had come to America in search of dollars. This change from the Edwardian procedure—when rich American girls would come to England in search of titles and all the grander appurtenances of "class"—marked the huge sea-change that World War I had created. Although Britain had won the war, and survived the revolutions that swept the continent, it was already clear, to those with foresight, that this was to be the American century.

During this first stay in New York, Noël's fortunes proved to be more elusive than he had expected, and his accommodation, which had started so grandly at the Algonquin, moved progressively downward into ever more humble circumstances. He was given a lifeline by Gabrielle Enthoven (a theater enthusiast who left a vast collection of theater memorabilia to the Theatre Museum, Covent Garden), who lent him her apartment for a short while.

During his 1924 stay, Noël decided to economize by moving to another friend's flat on East 32nd Street. When he returned to the city in 1926 he moved to the Gladstone on East 52nd Street—a smart but simpler base from which to operate.

He was in New York for the opening of his play, *This Was a Man*, but the rehearsals went so badly (as was often the case with his productions) that he decamped to Long Island. When the play opened on November 22 it was a failure. The old theatrical adage that a disastrous dress rehearsal meant a successful first night was not proved true on this occasion. Coward quipped to a friend that the actors' delivery of his script was so ploddingly slow that there was time to pop out and get an ice cream between each line!

Noël's next visit, in 1928, was a reconnaissance mission rather than a production, but he took the opportunity, during his two-week stay, to catch up with all the latest shows. On arrival he gave a press interview, in which he claimed that he felt perfectly at home in New York, whose theater-going public were much friendlier and more enthusiastic than those in London. Even allowing for a little judicious buttering-up of the local newspapers, Noël had put his finger on a truth that still holds good—Americans enjoy and applaud success, while the English are extremely wary of it.

The frenetic pace, the flaunting of wealth, the sense of fun, that characterized the New York of the 1920s was shattered by the Wall Street Crash in 1929. The knock-on effects reverberated around the world, and were reflected in the theater as well as other spheres of life. Noël was still writing comedies (most notably, of course, *Private Lives*), but there was an added depth and maturity to his work, as well as a sense of nostalgia and foreboding. *Cavalcade* was a patriotic tribute to the past, but also a warning about the future, a suggestion that there might be another *Titanic* disaster (there is a scene on board the doomed liner in the show) looming ahead.

Atlantic liners continued to convey Noël safely over the waves, however, and he chose to commemorate this international lifestyle by naming a production company, set up in the early '30s, "Trans-Atlantic Presentations." Recognizing the sense of owning his own place in New York he bought an apartment on East 52nd Street. But his stay there (in 1936) was brief, as he suffered one of his periodic bouts of nervous exhaustion. These were a characteristic of his career, and were, in a sense, a safety valve. He was so full of ideas, of energy, and of a ruthless determination to succeed that he lived life at a pace and intensity far greater than most of his contemporaries—which is, perhaps, why we remember him while they are long since forgotten.

It was to recover from these personal crises that he traveled abroad so often and in the luxurious and relaxing style of luxury ocean liners. Given that he divided his career between two of the greatest cities on earth, and given the phenomenal pace of life in New York, which was then, and still remains, the most exciting and vibrant metropolis on the planet, it is little wonder that these much needed holidays occurred so frequently.

When the world hit its equivalent of a collective breakdown, with the outbreak of World War II, Noël sailed to New York in order to arouse sympathy and support for Britain. He left for the U.S. in April 1940, shortly before the invasion and fall of France, which left Britain to face Nazi Europe alone. Officially, he was there to promote a new play (after all, the United States was a neutral country at the time) but the reality was that he was to be a one-man propaganda mission for England (rather as his friend and fellow composer/playwright, Ivor Novello, had been sent to Stockholm, in neutral Sweden, during World War I). The fact that he was able to enjoy unrationed food and a pre-war lifestyle in New York that was now just a memory in London was an added attraction.

Most of the restaurants he visited in those days for lunch or dinner no longer exist. The famous Le Pavillon, Le Voisin, Luchow's, the Colony restaurant, and the Cote Basque closed in 2004. These restaurants were very elegant except perhaps for Luchow's, which was more like a German steak house, often with a German band playing. Most of them were carpeted—Le Voisin, for example, was decorated with pale blue-gray walls, with pale gray carpeting, white plaster ceiling decorations, and small lamps with pale gray lamp-shades on each table, together with fresh flowers in crystal vases. The lighting was low and always very flattering to the ladies. While many cele-brated restaurants today have done away with carpeting in preference to bare wood, these restau-rants kept noise to the minimum and were con-sidered the more enjoyable because of it. The accounts in Coward's diaries, however, also men-tion the dinners he had in private homes, and it reads like a list from *Who's Who*. On Sunday, February 12, 1950, "In the evening dined at Guthrie's [McClintic] with Bob Hope, also Alec Guinness and Ruth Chatterton" (an American stage and film actress).

The war years saw Noël working in England and touring the Empire, with morale-boosting concerts for the troops. "Mad Dogs and Englishmen," one of Coward's best-known songs, played endlessly in troop concerts during World War II, a conflict in which he didn't take a direct part, but in which he did his bit on the silver screen, as a battleship captain (modelled on his friend, Lord Louis Mountbatten, in the film *In Which We Serve*.

Once the war had been safely won, however, he returned to America, but his *Tonight at 8:30* was not the success he had hoped for. The late 1940s and the 1950s were a very low period for Coward. Tastes had changed—the world had changed—and in many ways he seemed dated and out of touch. His big post-war musical, *Pacific 1860*, starring Mary

Martin, was a flop. What could he do? As the 1950s wore on, he had the added headache of income tax problems. The Labour government that had been elected by a landslide in 1945 had put taxes up to pay for a socialist transformation of the country. Noël was an unashamed Conservative, and was appalled by government politics as well as its economics, but it was the latter that hit the hardest.

What was he to do? At a time when America was at the height of its economic boom, it seemed that it might, as it had thirty years earlier, be a launching pad for his career. The growth of television (which was still relatively rare in England—it took the Queen's coronation in 1953 to kick-start it as a popular pastime in the United Kingdom) seemed to offer a solution, and Noël took the opportunity with both hands. He may have grown older and statelier, but at heart he was still the ambitious, determined man who had climbed from lower-middle-class obscurity to international fame and fortune.

Most of the money that Coward made in America came from appearing in cabaret in Las Vegas, and there is a famous record cover picture showing him standing, dressed in a tuxedo, in the Nevada desert. The idea for this work came from his having introduced Marlene Dietrich at the Café de Paris in London. If a huge star like her could, after the war, reinvent herself as a cabaret star, representing pre-war glamor and style, then so, in his way, could he.

In addition to Las Vegas cabaret, however, he also appeared on New York television, for CBS. And it was in New York that he met Mike Todd, the producer—and husband of Elizabeth Taylor. Todd persuaded him to take a part in *Around the World in Eighty Days* which starred David Niven, another Englishman famed for his old-world glamor and gentlemanly disposition. This was, sadly, to be Todd's only film, as he was killed in a plane crash not long afterward.

During the production of the TV show, Noël stayed in an apartment on East 54th Street—it had taken him twenty years to move two streets further towards the Upper East Side! The show, called *Together with Music*, was a great success, even though (or perhaps because) he had smoothed away some of the sexier lines in some of his songs, in deference to the rather more puritanical nature of American television audiences.

Tax troubles had led to Noël's working in America, and he decided to become a tax exile, as he had no intention of leading an impoverished old age. Much as he loved America, it was not the best place for him to live for this reason, so he bought homes in Bermuda (of which he tired) and then Switzerland, as well as his beloved Firefly, in Jamaica. It was while en route to Jamaica that he made his last ever journey to New York, in January 1973. Fittingly, he made his final public appearance on stage there, with his old friend Marlene Dietrich. After a week's residence in New York he traveled on to Jamaica, where he died two months later.

Coward's attitude to the States was summed up in the song "I Like America," but his love of New York could best be described, I feel, in the words of one of his comedy numbers: "I Went to a Marvellous Party." Noël may have died, but if his spirit lives on, one of the places at which it is to be found is surely at an after-theater party in the heart of Manhattan.

11

Legendary Figures of the Theater

Moss Hart was one of the most prominent figures in Broadway's golden age. He was a brilliant director and playwright, and knew everybody from the Algonquin Round Table group to the Gershwins, Irving Berlin, Noël Coward, Cole Porter, and Hollywood producers. His passion for the theater included his long play-writing collaboration with George S. Kaufman. Together they gave us such classic comedies as *You Can't Take it with You* and *The Man Who Came to Dinner*. On his own Hart wrote *Lady in the Dark* and *Light up the Sky*. He directed Julie Andrews in *My Fair Lady* and Richard Burton in *Camelot* as well as writing screenplays such as *A Star is Born* for Judy Garland. He wrote an autobiography called *Act One* which became a bestseller. His wife, Kitty Carlisle Hart, said one of their first dates was at 21. Dining out in legendary restaurants was part of his life and he was part of Broadway's musical theater as well as the legitimate stage. He died in 1961 at the age of fifty-seven.

Moss Hart's career spanned the broad spectrum of Broadway. He created, wrote, directed musicals, revues and straight plays. He had written a play called *I am Listening* and asked Katharine Cornell to play the lead. However, she was procrastinating and he was losing patience with her. One evening Noël Coward invited him to the Hotel Astor for the Allied Relief Ball, and there Moss met Gertrude Lawrence and decided that she was the ideal star for the part. Although Katharine Cornell was an excellent actress, he was overwhelmed by the talent of Gertie Lawrence. He took her to the Oak Room at the Plaza and over drinks he offered her the part. She nicknamed him "mossy-face" and then suggested that he change the title of the play, and that it would be much more appealing to call it, say, "Lady in the Dark." Steven Bach writes in his biography of Hart that he was always very extravagant and reckless with money; he liked to dine at the Plaza, Sardi's, Le Voisin, and 21 but business meetings often took place in the Oak Room at the Plaza.

At the beginning of his career he was fortunate enough to be asked to collaborate on a play with George S. Kaufman. Hart writes in his autobiography that he was told to go to Kaufman's house on East 63rd Street every day from 11 a.m. till 6 p.m. At the end of each working day, Hart embarrassed the sophisticated Kaufman by trying to thank him profusely for his interest and encouragement, but he had no idea that he was causing Kaufman a great deal of suffering by smoking cigars. However, Hart says Kaufman didn't know of the pain

Kaufman was inflicting on him: "The cause of my agony was simple enough. Mr. Kaufman cared very little about food." Work continued each day without lunch and Hart waited for tea to be brought in at 4 o'clock, which he said he could sniff coming up the stairs. He was tempted to gobble up everything on the tray, then to his great relief tea-time was moved up an hour earlier.

One day Kaufman announced that they would be having tea downstairs that day, as his wife was having people for tea. He thought that it would be a tea for a cousin or elderly aunt and was surprised when Kaufman's wife invited him too. Tea-time arrived and Moss was surprised by the number of voices coming from the room as they walked downstairs. He was in casual clothes, an old sports jacket and faded brown trousers. When he entered the room he was dumbstruck as he recognized everyone there and they were all celebrities. He said it was like one of those double-page murals in *Vanity Fair* of all the great figures of the theater and literary world. From Ethel Barrymore and Helen Hayes, Edna Ferber, George Gershwin, Harpo Marx to Alexander Woollcott. "Alfred Lunt—Moss Hart," said Mr. Kaufman. "Leslie Howard—Moss Hart;" he just managed to shake hands. "Get yourself a drink and bring Miss Parker one, will you?" said Kaufman. He heard someone begin to play the piano and thought it was George Gershwin except he couldn't see the piano—there were so many people in the room.

Returning home that evening he was even more determined to reach his goal in the theater and was "galvanised into a kind of working fury." When the play they were working on, *Once in a Lifetime*, was finished, auditions began at the Music Box Theater. After the grind and imprisonment of months in Kaufman's house, he wrote that it was bliss to be able to dash into the little drugstore next to the theater during the breaks and splurge on chocolate malteds and hamburgers. He never forgot those early years of starvation, or the theatrical feast, albeit a "tea," he had attended.

Continuing about legendary people in the theater who not only focused on their work but also food, one must not forget the Lunts. Alfred Lunt and Lynn Fontanne became known as "The Lunts" and in 1958 they had a theater named after them on Broadway. Alexander Woollcott wrote in 1924 that whoever saw the Lunts bowing hand in hand for the first time may well have been witnessing a moment in theatrical history. "It is among the possibilities that we are seeing the first chapter in a partnership destined to be as distinguished as that of Henry Irving and Ellen Terry." They were the first couple of the American theater for nearly fifty years, not only because they insisted on having dual billing, but as Lynn said, they mostly played lovers, so they were always in love. Lynn said, "One reason we lasted so long is that we usually played two people who were very much in love. As we were realistic actors,

we became these two people. So we had a diver-
tissement. I had an affair with him, and he
with me."

Lunt first courted Lynn at the boardinghouse
called Dr. Round's on West 70th Street, and this is
where Noël Coward used to visit them in 1924.
The three of them used to go to Laurette Taylor's
house parties at her home on Riverside Drive until
Taylor, jealous of Lynn's beauty and success,
began attacking Lynn verbally, much to Alfred's
anger. As Taylor began to have problems with
alcohol, many of her friends left her parties, never
to return.

Alfred Lunt began cooking for Lynn after they
were married, and he was concerned about her
health because she was so skinny. He cooked
breakfast which varied every day and this began
his life-long interest in cooking and preparing
dishes not only for Lynn but for guests who later
visited them in their country home. This home,
called Ten Chimneys, at Genesee Depot, 30 miles
west of Milwaukee, became a famous retreat from
Broadway, and they invited friends from all walks
of life to visit and stay with them. Julie Harris was
one. She said that the Lunts were not only great
actors, they were great human beings. Katharine
Hepburn said that every time she was visiting the
Lunts she was in a sort of a daze of wonder. The
dining room, the table, the china, the silver, the
food, the extraordinary care and beauty and taste
. . . a sort of dream, a vision.

Even though they were regarded as America's first couple, Lynn was born in England and grew up in Sussex. She said that the landscape around their country home reminded her of the Sussex countryside. Noël Coward often visited them there and the room in which he stayed is now called the Coward room. He wrote in his diary in New York in 1956, "This afternoon I'm going to the Lunts to be taught how to make pies."

During the war, they continued to help the war effort and in New York Alfred gave cooking lessons for the Theater Wing to raise money for the Stage Door Canteen. Lynn said that he was more nervous preparing to give a lesson than he was on a first night. He would lie in bed worrying about how he would conduct his next class and what recipes he would prepare.

In 1943 they went to London and played at the Aldwych Theatre during the Blitz. They had several narrow escapes and both the theater and the Savoy Hotel where they were staying were damaged by bombs. Later in 1957 when they were in Paris Alfred took a course at the Cordon Bleu Academy and received a diploma at the end, of which he was extremely proud.

During their time in the country he would often spend the day in the kitchen preparing dinner for his guests and was devastated if any dish wasn't exactly right. Guests would be treated like royalty and on departure would often be given a dozen fresh eggs to take with them.

Jared Brown in *The Fabulous Lunts* describes Alfred's specialities, including Norwegian fish balls, creamed baked potatoes, cardamom coffee bread, clam chowder, scrambled eggs with tomatoes, onions, chili sauce and Madeira, chicken livers with curry, broiled fillet of sole, turkey with a dry, simple stuffing made of a mixture of breadcrumbs and butter, onion, and sage. An elaborate dessert made of French ice cream in a coating of raspberry ice under a sauce comprised fresh crushed strawberries, Cointreau, grated orange peel and sugar, and Robert E. Sherwood's favorite, a combination of lamb, rice, mushrooms, and bacon. His wife Lynn didn't have as wide a range of dishes; however, her specialty, trifle for dessert, was apparently outstanding.

They knew everybody in the theater. Helen Hayes said that the Lunts were her idols, her teachers, her mentors, "that of all the lucky things that happened to me in my life in the theater the Lunts were the luckiest." Ten Chimneys was a home for the arts, literally and metaphysically.

Once when they were preparing to play in *The Guardsman* the plot troubled Alfred because of the improbability of a man being able to make his wife believe that he was someone else, even with an excellent disguise. He decided to try an experiment. He dressed in his costume and wearing make-up and using his new accent he decided to visit the grocer where he shopped every day. Lunt's great interest in cooking led to long conversations with this grocer, so he tried out his disguise. He carried on a lengthy discussion with the grocer and was delighted that he wasn't recognized, so he began rehearsals the following week with some relief.

They both retired in the 1960s. Alfred died in 1977 followed by Lynn in 1983. They are still regarded as the greatest of the American theater, and since the re-opening of Ten Chimneys their legend lives on.

Another theater legend who focused a good deal on food, mainly because of his health, was the actor Yul Brynner.

I was the personal assistant to Yul Brynner during his final tour of *The King and I*; after traveling across the country he made his farewell appearances in New York. It was then that the experience of actually dining with legends became a reality. Yul Brynner seemed to know all the great stars of Hollywood and Broadway, and you never knew who would come backstage to see him after the show. Often they would accompany him to dinner afterward, sometimes to a night club but usually to one of his favorite restaurants.

I had heard that some actors carry their own food with them. Very few stars carry around their own food, except for Carol Channing who carries hers in a vacuum flask. Yul Brynner traveled with his own cook and therefore had to have a hotel suite with a kitchen plus several pounds of carrots awaiting them on arrival, so that Mr. B. could have freshly prepared carrot juice. He already had cancer and his doctor told him to drink large quantities of it every day.

The experience of working with Brynner and having to follow his instructions, especially about his eating habits, triggered my first thoughts about celebrities dining out, particularly performers such as Noël Coward who was a friend of Yul's, and in fact was offered the part of the King of Siam and turned it down before it was offered to Yul Brynner.

When I got the job I realized I was about to enter the world of a "superstar," a rarefied world of limousines, security guards, paparazzi, orchids delivered daily, Trump Tower accommodation, and celebrity-studded evenings. I met more celebrated actors while working for Mr. B. than I could ever have imagined. Like Moss Hart and Noël Coward, he knew everybody and everybody knew him. He had had a long career in Hollywood as well as on Broadway.

Laurence Olivier captured Broadway when the Old Vic company made their triumphant tour to New York just after the war. The cast list, perhaps the most illustrious in history, was headed by Olivier, Ralph Richardson, Alec Guinness, and Sybil Thorndike. The company was the toast of Broadway, and ever since then British actors have made an indelible mark on the American scene. Olivier said that the 1945/46 season was the one that "made our names. The reception was as happy as a marriage bell." However, they found that costs in New York were much higher than they had anticipated, and the actors were beginning to get hungry.

Vivien Leigh accompanied him on the tour, and they stayed at the St. Regis Hotel on West 55th Street. In his book he says he was worried about finances even though they were taking Broadway by storm. "It was natural for the two of us to stay at the St. Regis; it would have been misunderstood if we had sought somewhere more economical." ("God, these English have lost all their standards since the war." David O. Selznick did actually say those words about the British a year later.) People who saw those performances still vividly remember them. It was the continuation of a love affair between American audiences and the British classical theater. Most of the productions to follow would be the classics, Shakespeare, Ibsen, Shaw, done by the new National Theatre and the Royal Shakespeare Company.

Olivier was conscious about having the luck of the devil. "I wanted to make something of a name as an actor. I suppose I can say I have," he said in September 1946.

I wanted to have a house in the country . . . Now . . . I think I can honestly say that I would like to "give" something to the theater instead of taking something out of it . . . I would like to help found . . . a steady and strong Old Vic Company . . . so steady and strong that it doesn't matter a bit if either I or Ralph Richardson or anyone else retires from it. Something that stands on its own feet and can tell us both to go to hell.

In 1958 Olivier arrived in New York with the play *The Entertainer*, and according to Hugo Vickers in his biography of Vivien Leigh it was then that his affair with Joan Plowright became serious, as she was in the cast playing his daughter. Noël Coward had dinner at Sardi's with Olivier after the show one evening during the run on Broadway, and he told Coward he couldn't really take living with Vivien any longer. It was the beginning of the end of the marriage.

Richard Burton started his career in London, and played most of the great Shakespearean roles either at Stratford-on-Avon or at the Old Vic. He could hold the audience in the palm of his hand, and his voice was one of the finest in the British theater. It is instantly recognizable even years after his death. He was seduced by Hollywood and Elizabeth Taylor. However, he did continue to act on Broadway, but never returned to the Old Vic or the National. He made several appearances on Broadway before he played Hamlet there in 1964, directed by John Gielgud.

His *Hamlet* was sold out, and the Broadway tradition of a standing ovation for a Brit playing Shakespeare on Broadway was followed. He and Julie Andrews were a fire-cracker combination in *Camelot*, for although Burton could sing about as well as Rex Harrison, his charisma enchanted every-body. Masses of fans waited for him outside every night, and a story, perhaps true, tells that one snowy night, he spotted a couple leaving the performance early to grab a cab: He watched them depart and shouted from the stage "Get one for me too."

A drama producer at the BBC said, "He speaks the English language better than almost anybody else." Richard Harris, a close friend, said "Half of him wanted to be the best actor in the world. The other half didn't care enough."

His role of King Arthur in *Camelot* was a great success. He loved the challenge. "It sounds perverse," he admitted, "but when you're given a perfectly written part, like Hamlet, there's not much you can do with it after the first few performances. The Burton Hamlet is the Burton Hamlet and that's that. But in a show like Camelot when the changes are coming thick and fast with the re-writes, all things are possible. You can make something of the part that is yours and yours alone." His co-star, Julie Andrews, was now well-known to Broadway audiences, and her reputation as a world-wide international star was firmly established.

Burton's brother, Graham Jenkins, went to New York for Burton's final night in *Camelot*. He recalls that at the farewell party, Moss Hart, the Broadway director, led the toast. "Great actors like you," he said to Burton, "are born once in a lifetime. You are as big a personality off the stage as on the stage, and you are, in every sense, larger than life.

I beg you not to waste your wonderful gifts. You must know you have it in you to be one of the greatest stage actors of this century." His brother continues with the words, "Sadly, this plea was only heard. It was not understood."

When Burton played in Peter Shaffer's play *Equus* twelve years later, the celebrated agent Robby Lantz said, "He revitalized not just the play but the whole of Broadway. In what had been a lackluster season, business picked up all around." His last appearance on Broadway was with Elizabeth Taylor in Noël Coward's play *Private Lives*. The pre-opening publicity was enormous, and it was the show business event of the season. However, the critics panned the production even though all the performances sold out.

In 1984, when he died, at his memorial service, the actor George Segal who was his co-star in the film *Who's Afraid of Virginia Woolf?* said, "There is nothing in my life that comes close to the experience of working with Richard Burton. We have always known, those of us who act, that he was the best one. He makes us all proud to be actors."

Burton acted in Dylan Thomas's play *Under Milk Wood* several times and he appeared in a reading at the Old Vic with other well-known Welsh actors including Emlyn Williams and Rachel Roberts.

Dylan Thomas worked at the BBC, sometimes freelance and also as a member of the staff. He went to America in 1950 on his first tour, giving readings of his works across the States. He was on his fourth visit when he died in New York of alcoholic poisoning. The Chelsea Hotel was where he stayed in Manhattan, and there is a plaque outside the front door in his memory. His favorite drinking spot was the White Horse Tavern in Greenwich Village, but it was at the Chelsea Hotel that he spent his last days.

John Gielgud of course is unforgettable. He was an enormous success on Broadway both acting and directing. He writes that it is certainly a great advantage, if one's acting is to remain in people's memories for maybe fifty years or so. It does largely depend on the roles they played. Charles Hawtrey and Gerald du Maurier were both brilliant artists, but they rarely played very ambitious roles and therefore the public scarcely remembers them now they are gone. Gielgud and Ralph Richardson scored the greatest hit of their later life starring in Harold Pinter's play, *No Man's Land*, on Broadway in 1976. Gielgud noted rather sadly, "Ralph always insists on the best restaurants, whereas I seem to eat out of tins, rather like Edith Evans who shows her heart and then slams it shut again."

Robert Morley was another charismatic actor who conquered Broadway. In 1948 he opened at the Martin Beck Theater in his own play *Edward My Son*. Brook Atkinson in the *New York Times* wrote, "He is an actor in the grand manner; imposing and deliberate, with a broad sweep to his style of expression. But on the big surfaces he can give you some exquisitely neat details, for he is also witty and droll, a master of satiric inflections. He is downright superb."

Morton Gottlieb was the general manager of the company which was composed of mostly English actors. Robert began inviting people to his dressing room for tea. He had two dressing rooms; one was by the stage to enable him to make quick changes. On matinée days, during the break he would not only invite Peggy Ashcroft, his co-star, but everybody from dressers to stagehands. He provided the tea and everyone had to take turns to bring cookies and cake. Then the actors in other shows in the area started to come over on matinée days and have tea.

This dressing room became the secret hot spot during Broadway matinées. Nine years later, Helen Hayes revived the tradition when she was in a production of *Time Remembered* with Richard Burton and Susan Strasberg. Except she asked the four musicians who were in the show to go backstage to play for them; it was a full-blown revival. Robert Morley's distinct, brilliant style of comedy will long be remembered. Elizabeth Taylor also brought great charisma to Broadway. During the time that Richard Burton was playing Hamlet, she would go to the theater every night and be mobbed at the stage door. Hundreds of people would stop traffic in Times Square just to get a glimpse of her.

Broadway audiences still remember John Gielgud, Laurence Olivier, Richard Burton, Rex Harrison, and Robert Morley as the British stars who captured New York by their charisma.

Among home-grown talent Helen Hayes used to provide feasts for fellow actors at her country home on weekends and showed off her lovely garden, Kim Hunter whose best-known role was Stella in Tennessee Williams' play *A Streetcar Named Desire* wrote a cookbook called *Loose in the Kitchen* in her free time, and Laurette Taylor was a very popular hostess in New York as well as being one of the foremost actresses of the twentieth century. She inspired Noël Coward to create one of his most memorable stage characters, Judith Bliss. She met English playwright Hartley Manners and after a courtship of two years they married. Although very happily married she engaged in a passionate dalliance with the film star John Gilbert. She began to drink heavily, and her relationship to real life continued to be a problem. When Hartley Manners died of cancer, his death was a tremendous blow and Laurette went into a period of retirement. In 1945 she gave her last performance in Tennessee Williams' *The Glass Menagerie*, which won her great acclaim, and the playwright's life-long admiration. She died in New York City in 1946.

12

Theatrical Nibbles and Nuggets

Americans knew Alistair Cooke best as the elegant host of *Masterpiece Theater* on Public Television. But in Britain, where he was born, he was known almost exclusively for his weekly BBC radio program *Letter from America*. He told the story about being in the restaurant at the famous Carlyle Hotel several years ago. He was about to tuck into his lobster bisque when a stranger stopped at the table and said, "You look familiar, do I know you?"

"I'm Bob Hope," Mr. Cooke replied.

The intruder backed off in confusion and Mr. Cooke returned to his soup, chuckling softly. "I've used that since my TV days, works every time. They know I'm not Hope but they don't know what else to say." He has touched every aspect of American life in his letters, from major events like the civil rights movement, the Vietnam War, and the small but not so significant happenings that help to illustrate who Americans are and how they think.

One of his favorite actresses, then working on Broadway, was the British actress Jessica Tandy, who became more famous in the United States for her roles in the theater and in film than in Britain.

She was married to the late Hume Cronyn and they lived not far from Alistair and his wife. One of her great successes on Broadway was the famous production of *A Streetcar Named Desire*. The play opened at the Ethel Barrymore Theater on December 3, 1947. Tandy and Brando were contracted to play the first two years. "Certainly Marlon didn't sustain the long run," said Tandy:

He would be brilliant one night, and the next night, if he was tired or bored, he would play tired or bored. He didn't have the discipline. I used to get very cross at him. It's hard to do a long run. But Karl Malden was disciplined; Kim Hunter was disciplined; I was disciplined; and Marlon was not. It used to drive me mad that every time he slammed that telephone down, he would break it. And the prop man was going mad.

Then there was the scene where we were sitting at the table having a meal, and he would slam down the cup! And always on the key word of what I was saying. Now, Marlon was not doing that on purpose. But I did at one point say, "Look, if you're going to slam it down, slam it down. But not on my key word." It was difficult enough to be heard in that theater anyway, because of the air-conditioning units that made such a noise in the balcony.

Elia Kazan, the director of the play, bawled him out one day, because Kazan had called a rehearsal for the two of us, to take out some of the "improvements," I guess. The first time Kazan did that, Marlon came very late. The second time, he didn't show at all. He simply forgot. It's not as if Marlon was aiming to be spiteful or malicious, because there wasn't a mean bone in his body. But Kazan apparently bawled him out, and said, "You better apologize to her." So Marlon wrote me a letter of apology. And I cared enough about him to write one back in which I said that I thought he had the capacity to be to America what Olivier was in England, but that he wasn't helping himself.

I really cared a lot about him. He was a brilliant stage actor. But after *Streetcar* he never returned to the stage. I don't think he liked acting. I remember, he told me he would never make the movie. Of course, that was practically the first thing he did. And we can all be thankful for the many wonderful performances he's given since.

The great danger of a long run is that you can allow yourself to be led away from your performance by an audience. One night the audience will laugh at something, and another night they won't. You then ask yourself, "What did I do wrong?" Now you try harder. An insecure actor will kill his performance, because he will try to repeat that result rather than to simply play the play. You must not worry about "How am I doing?" That's the pitfall. Instead, you must sustain a performance by concentrating on the author's intention, the director's intention and your own knowledge to the part.

Rex Harrison's approach to the audience during a long run, such as *My Fair Lady*, was a little more confident. He could sustain his performance by his technique, as well as have the ability to ad lib and improvise during any performance.

Tea matinées were a very popular event up to the early 1970s. At one, a parsimonious couple wishing to save their leftovers, presumably to be consumed at curtain fall, perched their tea tray on the front of the stage. As the curtain rose after the intermission, and without a pause in the proceedings, Sexy Rexy helped himself to the pot of tea and what was left of the cucumber sandwiches, and munched and sipped his way to the end of the scene, much to the delight of the audience and the couple's amazement.

Brian Cox, the British actor who has played on Broadway several times, tells this story about Sir Alec Guinness. Sir Alec gave this advice to him when he was a student: "The audience is an unruly beast, to be tamed and kept firmly in its place." Sir Alec was no slouch at following his own advice. The first was a performance of *The Cocktail Party* by T.S. Eliot. During a duologue of a particularly quiet intensity, there was an outbreak of mass coughing. Sir Alec's method of dealing with this was to mimic the seizure. He literally coughed the audience into a submissive and embarrassed silence.

Another occasion was when he was playing Shakespeare's Scottish King. On his first entrance, some old dear in the front row had the temerity to check her program across the footlights to see who had just entered. Sir Alec made a beeline downstage and judiciously, with his right foot, booted the program out of her hands.

One of Sir Alec's favorite restaurants was Le Veau d'Or on East 60th Street. He made so many trips to New York his second favorite restaurant was on the *Q.E.2*.

Many theatrical feasts in New York are fundraisers, where Broadway stars give their free evenings to appear for charity. Sam Wanamaker arranged dozens of these when fundraising for the Globe Theatre Guild. Wealthy donors or potential donors would host an elegant supper party after which a group of famous theatrical folk would entertain. Ian McKellen did his one-man Shakespeare show in the presence of Princess Grace of Monaco, and in 2003 Barry Day arranged a program to raise funds for the New Globe Theatre to be built in an old fort on Governor's Island, which is next door to Staten Island.

Barry Day has written a brilliant book, *This Wooden O*, about Sam Wanamaker rebuilding the Globe Theatre in London, so obviously he is interested in the new Globe Theater in New York. He writes that when Sam was looking for more financing he always turned to America. This wasn't Sam's first foray into fundraising but it was the most serious to date. He now needed to attract and focus serious transatlantic attention on the project and he didn't want to be seen as the impecunious swain with his hand out. The idea of a troupe of wandering players seemed particularly appropriate.

The speech Sam rehearsed for one such event was Prospero's soliloquy from *The Tempest* put to music as a two-hander for Douglas Fairbanks, Jr., and jazz singer Cleo Laine. The evening arrived and the strolling players had a core group of Laine and her husband, John Dankworth, Fairbanks, Millicent Martin, Michael York, and Nicol Williamson (who turned out to have a singing voice pleasantly reminiscent of Hoagy Carmichael). The audiences loved mingling with the celebrities, and the contributions began to come in—"although we never asked for money," Sam was quick to point out.

Very occasionally he got more than he bargained for. John Dankworth recalls three silver-haired ladies approaching Sam and asking nervously: "We're just three little widows, but if we make up a half a million dollars between us, would you accept it?"

In 2003 I organized theatrical feasts at the Algonquin Hotel as fund-raisers for the English-Speaking Union in New York. Although we did not have an offer of half a million dollars, we have had some celebrated guests taking part, including Rosemary Harris and Roger Moore. Guests have dinner in the dining room, some of them sitting at the Round Table, followed by a performance in the Oak Room. In a tribute to Noël Coward, Roger Moore spoke of his work in a Coward play, and that the reason he was in New York at the time was to be the mystery guest in the play *The Play What I Wrote* by Hamish McColl and Sean Foley.

During the last few years some of the most popular British celebrities ever in New York have left us but their reputations will live on. The Beatles' arrival in Manhattan will never be forgotten, and they certainly didn't order pea sandwiches at their New York hotel, which they did when they were staying at the Savoy in London. Dudley Moore will be remembered for his drunk scene arriving and during dinner at the Plaza Hotel in the film *Arthur*. Quentin Crisp, one of the most charismatic Brits in New York, died in 1999. It is remarkable to remember how much impact they created in the States.

In 2000 Barry Humphries as Dame Edna Everage scored a great hit at the Booth Theater on Broadway with his one-man show, *Dame Edna: The Royal Tour*. It was interesting to see if the show would appeal to American audiences, as one of his earlier shows over a decade ago had failed in New York. However, the critics loved him and he successfully toured the rest of the States after the Broadway run. Part of his show in New York was to invite two people from the audience to eat dinner on stage while he was performing. He brought on a small table and two chairs and as the

Booth Theater is almost next door to Sardi's, each evening a waiter from Sardi's would arrive half-way through the show and serve them dinner. It was rather unusual to watch two people eating dinner reluctantly under the gaze of the audience and Dame Edna.

Another performer who has had a great success in the past few years is comedian Jackie Mason in his show *Prune Danish*. Many of his jokes are about food and what people eat before or after the theater. One of his favorite places is the Carnegie Deli on Seventh Avenue and 55th Street. This deli is famous for its giant three-inch-deep sandwiches filled with hot pastrami, turkey or chicken, ham and cheese with many different kinds of breads. On weekends there is always a queue to get in. Another recent trend is for "theme" restaurants where the queues are even longer. Jekyll and Hyde on Sixth Avenue at 58th Street has skeletons hanging around the front door with more grue-some decorations inside. They serve mostly fast foods including hamburgers and steak sandwiches, as does Planet Hollywood and The Hard Rock Café on West 57th Street.

Quentin Crisp, Resident Alien in New York, gave an interview to Gyles Brandreth in Manhattan shortly before he died. Gyles said:

I had lunch with Quentin Crisp the week before he died. We met in the Bowery Bar on the Lower East Side for crabcakes and whiskey, and for two hours I sat and gazed in wonder at an old man with mauve hair, the self-styled "Stately homo of England" as—head held high and almost in profile—he talked, in a gravelly, lilting voice about life, death and his vision of the great hereafter.

I think I will like the food in Heaven. I like food that tastes of nothing and I'm sure that's what they serve. Here, I eat most of my meals in the Cooper Diner on Second Avenue, where you can eat anything and it all tastes the same. I don't like kinky food. As you go up Second Avenue, you pass Thai restaurants, Tibetan restaurants, Chinese, Indian, but it all tastes very peculiar, so I avoid it. Usually I eat alone; I go to most places alone. When I receive an invitation I go, and if you can live on peanuts and champagne you need never buy food in New York. I am content with my fate.

13

Critics' Flavors

It is interesting to note that P.G. Wodehouse, Kenneth Tynan, and Frank Rich were all drama critics in New York at one stage of their lives, yet their tastes and backgrounds were vastly different. You could have found P.G. Wodehouse eating while trading quips with Dorothy Parker in the 1920s at the Algonquin among fine china and crystal, you could perhaps find Kenneth Tynan in the 1970s drinking in the King Cole Room at the St. Regis, and Frank Rich in the 1990s eating steak at Gallagher's, where they still hang joints of raw meat in the front windows of the restaurant. Frank Rich was the drama critic for the *New York Times* and could close a show with his review, which earned him the name of "The Butcher of Broadway."

These three men wrote the most influential reviews of the Broadway theater. P.G. Wodehouse worked as a drama critic on the *New Yorker* before Dorothy Parker took his job. Years later Kenneth Tynan wrote for the same magazine.

P.G. Wodehouse was born in Guildford, Surrey, U.K. No doubt he was brought up on typically English food, from shepherd's pie and spotted dick to roast beef and yorkshire pudding on Sundays. This cuisine is certainly not what he would have found in America. However, he obviously knew about haute cuisine, because he wrote about the aristocracy, class distinctions, butlers, and gentlemen burglars, all of whom would have totally different tastes in food, from caviar to fish and chips.

He first visited New York in 1904 for a few weeks holiday, when he was twenty-three. He had just left a tediously boring job in a bank, and in one of his books he wrote "Why America? I have often wondered about that. Why, I mean, from my earliest years was it America that was always to me the land of romance? It is not as though I had been intoxicated by cowboys or Indians, but I had this yearning I had to visit America."

That same year Wodehouse became involved with the theater. He was asked to write an extra lyric for a show in London and his friend Guy Bolton knew he had a good ear for music. As a result of a successful song, the actor Seymour Hicks offered him a job at the Aldwych Theatre as a lyricist to write extra material when needed for a number of musical comedies, and to adapt verses and songs. A friend who was with him at the time said, "On leaving the stage door, Wodehouse was so stunned with joy and excitement that we walked a mile along the Strand without him knowing where he was or whether he was coming or going." The composer he was to work with was Jerome Kern, and thus began a collaboration some years later of Kern and Wodehouse.

After 1909 he traveled regularly to New York. He wrote a play called *A Gentleman of Leisure*, and the gentleman burglar, the lead, was Douglas Fairbanks Sr., then appearing in *Chicago* by John Barrymore. It was the first play of its kind that was set on both sides of the Atlantic.

In 1915 he was in New York and met up again with Jerome Kern and Guy Bolton. They became a team and produced an incredible run of hit shows. They were the toast of Broadway. Wodehouse's work was praised to the skies and his lyrics composed at this time included the famous song "Bill" from *Showboat*. Wodehouse became the drama critic for *Vanity Fair* and Dorothy Parker succeeded him. She wrote "You could get a seat for their hit show *Oh, Lady, Lady!* for just about the price of one on the Stock Exchange." Besides *Oh Lady, Lady!* there were seven or eight other hit shows including *Oh Boy* (1917), renamed *Oh Joy* in London, with Beatrice Lillie, and *Oh Kay* with Gertie Lawrence. George and Ira Gershwin wrote the music and lyrics for this one, but Kern and Wodehouse wrote the book and also part of *Anything Goes*. *Oh Kay* was a hit on both sides of the Atlantic.

It is interesting to note the way he worked with Jerome Kern. Wodehouse said that Jerome usually wrote the music first and then he would add the words. That way he could see the musical high spots in it, and could fit the high spots to the lyric. W.S. Gilbert, of Gilbert and Sullivan fame, argued with this and said the words should come first. Wodehouse's talent was not in writing lyrics which read as light verse but in fitting the words to the tune. Unfortunately these musical comedies are no longer produced, but Broadway still remembers those hits. Ira Gershwin, Cole Porter, and Noël Coward all recognized Wodehouse's unique style, although hardly any of his lyrics have survived.

Wodehouse was criticized for being in America during World War I. However, he had trouble with his eyes, which excused him—although his public did not know this fact. His greatest successes were in New York in the 1920s, and people such as Noël Coward and Gertie Lawrence would have been vastly impressed with the huge hit he was on the other side of the "pond." He crossed the Atlantic frequently, to enable him to work on productions both in New York and London.

In New York he was introduced to celebrities who wined and dined him in the legendary restaurants such as the 21 Club and Sardi's. His British characers were aristocratic; he wrote about their hugely expensive way of life, and their interest in gourmet food, which also included their knowledge of the best French wines for dinner, the best months to eat game or oysters. He must have found the cuisine in New York quite different in the fact that people drank hard liquor with their meals, often declining wine for another double Scotch to wash down their steaks, the Scotch often being served from teapots during the Prohibition period.

His nickname was Plum, and in January 1929 his daughter wrote an article about him for the *Strand Magazine*, saying that he had an overwhelming horror of being bored, and an overpowering hatred of hurting people. It is unusual that a writer whose subjects seem so much attuned to British readers should have had so much success in America. However, the Americans have always had an interest in British writing. The common language, the fact that historically the Americans were of British stock, and the traditional colonial inferiority complex made many of them consider work emanating from England superior to what was written in the United States. The turn-of-the-century habit of U.S. heiresses marrying English aristocrats is another example of this veneration of their English roots.

Another British star on Broadway was the critic Kenneth Tynan. He became the theater critic for the *New Yorker* magazine (1958–60) and he championed the new realism of John Osborne and Arnold Wesker. His time in New York is recorded brilliantly in his late wife's biography of him. In 1961 he produced on Broadway *Oh Calcutta!* the all-nude show which shocked most of New York. It was nearly closed down by the police but then went on to make millions, although Tynan received only a small percentage. His work as a critic was taken much more seriously. John Lahr was given the same job at the *New Yorker* in 1992 by Tina Brown. He writes, "In American theatrical circles the definition of a genius is anybody from England."

The *New Yorker* commented: "Tynan's entries remain sharp and stylish to the end, as his wit, rage, and ambition jockey for position." Most theater people remember Tynan's brilliant career in London, where he wrote drama reviews for the *Observer* and other papers for many years, as well as being the Literary Manager at the Old Vic Theatre when Laurence Olivier was running the company.

When he was invited to be the drama critic on the *New Yorker*, he left London for the Broadway scene. The other writers at the magazine admired his work tremendously and the later drama critic John Lahr collected and edited the diaries of Kenneth Tynan. Lahr writes in his introduction that "Tynan's performance of personality—the flamboyant dress (dove-gray suits and velvet collars, pastel shirts), mannerisms (cigarette held between the third and fourth finger), and word-horde—embraced the notion of the extraordinary that he'd studied on stage and screen." As well as his work as a critic, he began a series of "Profiles" for the magazine, and they unabashedly reflected his taste and bias: actors, directors, and writers, from Ralph Richardson and Nicol Williamson to Louise Brooks and Mel Brooks.

Tynan writes in his profile of Noël Coward that they had a rather unusual meeting in Sardi's restaurant one evening. It was after curtain time on Broadway and the restaurant was relatively empty. Tynan was eating alone and he suddenly saw Coward come in, also alone. That very morning Tynan had printed a devastating review about Coward's latest play, an adaptation of Feydeau called *Look after Lulu*. Tynan writes that no sooner than Coward had taken his seat than he spotted him. Coward rose at once and "came padding across the room to the table behind which I was cringing. With eyebrows quizzically arched and upper lip raised to unveil his teeth, he leaned towards me. 'Mr. T.,' he said crisply, 'you are a c**t. Come and have dinner with me.' Not once did he mention the notice or the play. It would have been easy to cut or to crush me. It was typical of Coward that he chose, with an almost certain flop on his hands, to amuse and advise me instead."

In Tynan's profile of Nicol Williamson he describes the almost manic behavior of the actor when he was working in New York, especially when he arrived from England to prepare for a performance at the White House. A great deal of drinking and carousing went on at some of the best watering holes in Manhattan. For some reason Tynan seemed to be in charge of his preparing and delivering his one-man show on this occasion. Tynan wrote: "The reason is that during this period of our association I tried to 'drink for' Nicol, as I phrased it to myself. When he ordered wine, I would consume as much of it myself as I discreetly could, in order to keep his energies fresh for rehearsal. I do not know whether this unselfishness was of any real use to him. It nearly crippled me."

Frank Rich was the drama critic for the *New York Times* from 1980 to 1993. He began going to see Broadway plays with his mother when they would travel up to New York from Washington and stay overnight. In his biography *Ghost Light*, he recalls staying at the huge old Astor Hotel, now demolished, on Times Square, in a room which faced right out over Shubert Alley. On one visit, his mother gave him a $10 bill and allowed him to go out for dinner alone before meeting her at a nearby theater before the show. Rich decided to go to Frankie and Johnnie's restaurant on 45th Street. Walking up the stairs to the restaurant he felt a thrill at being so independent. At the table his feet didn't touch the ground, and the waiter asked if he wanted the children's menu. "No," he said, he wanted the regular menu which was like a huge piece of cardboard that folded up like a box. He collected playbills (programs), read the *Variety* show business paper and seeing the Broadway stars on stage became his *raison d'être*, and led him to become years later one of New York's foremost critics. He usually liked the British plays imported from the West End.

David Hare's and Christopher Hampton's plays have been equally successful on Broadway, although it was one of David Hare's, *The Secret Rapture*, that received a bad notice from Rich. After the review the play closed after nineteen previews and twelve performances. Hare retaliated and wrote back to him. His letter was circulated, attacking Rich for irresponsible nastiness, and for single-handedly closing his play. *Variety* hailed Hare's attack under a banner headline "Ruffled Hare Airs Rich Bitch." They agreed with the playwright, and accused Rich of a spree of negative reviews and sarcastic notices, and of being the cause of increasing resentment in the trade. Hare asked to meet him; Rich wrote back, but refused to meet Hare: "Next time you're in New York, why not spend less time meeting with critics, or attempting to, and more time seeing the plays your audience is seeing. You may learn more about why your play closed." He added, "The *Times* did not close your play . . . the producers closed your play."

Rich also panned a production of *The Tempest* with Frank Langella playing the role of Prospero. The director, Jude Kelly, came from Britain with a big reputation, but all the New York critics seemed to agree that her low-key production was a letdown, and lacked true Shakespearean authority.

Hare's complaint is a common one on Broadway, but it is seldom heard so publicly. Basically the objection is that the *New York Times* is so influential that its critic can close a show. Hare told

Variety, "I think Rich is totally irresponsible in the use of his power." *Variety* commented, "Rich's exceptionally harsh review of the Hare play, which drew favorable reviews from other critics, guaranteed its box office doom."

Clive Barnes, the British critic who has had a long career in New York, reporting not only as a drama critic but as a dance critic, is far more popular than Frank Rich. He says:

> I have a great deal of fellow sympathy for Rich. The lot of the *New York Times* drama critic is not a happy one—and the sense of responsibility can be insufferably heavy, especially as you are powerless to do anything about it. . . . Indeed, when I had the job it wasn't even particularly well paid (it's probably better now) and there were certainly more kicks than ha'pennies.
>
> It is difficult to know what could be done to lessen the critics' power in New York. A few of us might have acerbic tongues but generally speaking we are milder, softer, and gentler than our London colleagues. But more powerful. Why?

The Irish playwright Brendan Behan, visiting New York in connection with the production of *The Hostage* (1969), also was vulnerable to the critics, and he wrote:

> A Broadway author—I am proud to call myself one—always waits, on the first night of his play,

either in Sardi's or Downey's, and his press agent goes out to get the six newspapers, which are called "the Six Butchers of Broadway."

Now if you get six out of six good reviews, you could ask the President of the United States to sell you the White House, though I don't think this has ever happened. If you get five good reviews, you are doing fairly well and you have to start worrying about 480 Lexington Avenue, which is the home of the income tax. It is not a bad kind of worry though in its own way, if you have got to have worries, and I suppose everyone has to have them. If you have four, you can afford to give a party, or at least you can afford to attend the party which is usually given for you.

If you get three good reviews, it's time to go home to bed, but if you only get two, you stay there the whole of the following day and don't go to your hotel until after dark. If you get one good review, you just make an air reservation very quickly to get back to where you came from, but if you get six bad reviews, you take a sleeping pill. You might even take an overdose!

However I think I got five or six good reviews. Enough to keep me in business anyway. I know Walter Kerr of the *New York Herald-Tribune* and Howard Taubman of the *New York Times* were both enthusiastic over *The Hostage* and they are the really important reviewers. No, I forget. They are all important. I will be writing another play!

Actually, I got pretty good reviews and when I went into Sardi's that night, the crowd stood up and clapped.

Frank Rich is no longer drama critic at the *New York Times*, and he has written his childhood memoir—which reveals his early ambitions to be involved in the theater world—called *Ghost Light*. There is a superstition that if an empty theater is ever left completely dark, a ghost will take up residence. To prevent this, a single "ghost light" is left burning at center stage after the audience and all of the actors and musicians have gone home. Rich has certainly left his own ghost in many of the theaters where he killed the productions within.

14

Modern Stars . . . or Sugar and Spice

Lynn, Vanessa, and Corin Redgrave, Eileen Atkins, and the late Alan Bates regularly work on Broadway as does Maggie Smith, and now the younger Redgrave family including Natasha and Joely Richardson are joining them, with Liam Neeson, Brian Cox, and Alan Cumming.

Tom Conti says: "Being in a hit play on Broadway is one of the most exciting things that can happen to an actor. There is much more of a family feeling between the performers than in London. During my season there, Lucy Arnaz and I, on Saturdays, organized an event called Matinée Idles where cast members from various productions would eat together between shows."

Robert Stephens (late ex-husband of Maggie Smith), in his autobiography *Knight Errant*, co-written with Michael Coveney, said that if you are successful in New York the world is your oyster, and everyone is after you. He writes that Albert Finney once told him that when he was in a play on Broadway he received a phone call from a well-known actress in California, who said that she was coming to see the play, and then to see him afterwards. He had never met her in his life. She flew into New York, saw the play, saw Albert, took him to bed, and then flew home again. Stephens said that nobody actually flew that far for a night in bed with him, but that he was propositioned by Marlene Dietrich at a party in New York.

Earlier, in 1954, Julie Andrews went to New York in *The Boyfriend*. Then followed *My Fair Lady* in 1956 and *Camelot* in 1960. She was then whisked off to Hollywood stardom both in musical and non-musical films. Her long-awaited return to Broadway didn't happen till 1995, in a stage version of *Victor/Victoria*, and she received an unprecedented outpouring of affection from critics and audience alike. Julie Andrews says that she was fortunate enough to be in at the very end of that great, golden era on Broadway. But one thing she does agree that has changed for the better is that today one can use body mikes to help save one's voice. When she was playing in *My Fair Lady* for more than three years it was killing, an endurance test. Also, because of the extreme heat of the summer in New York, theaters must be air-conditioned, and therefore you have to use a mike to overcome the noise of the machine.

Jean Marsh recalls that they asked to have the air-conditioning turned off in the theater, but then she nearly fainted with the heat. She had been in New York working as an actress before the TV series

Upstairs Downstairs, but she did not have very much work and returned to Britain, only to be "discovered" after the series was aired. In 1979 she starred with Tom Conti on Broadway in *Whose Life is it, Anyway?* She had already been seen in 1957 in *Much Ado about Nothing* with John Gielgud.

Even though she had a star role she tells of the cramped backstage conditions. There was a little warren of dressing rooms. Hers was on the second floor landing of a back stairway, not much bigger than a closet with dreams of grandeur. In 1975 she was in Alan Bennett's *Habeas Corpus* with Rachel Roberts, Donald Sinden, June Havoc, and Celeste Holm. However, the New York-based British critic Clive Barnes gave it a bad review, and Bennett said that he was glad Barnes doesn't operate in London.

Broadway audiences were fully aware of what was happening in London, and when the new kitchen-sink dramas of the 1950s and '60s became successful, they too went to New York. *Look Back in Anger* transferred, followed by the new plays of Osborne, Storey, Wesker, and Alan Bennett. Albert Finney, Tom Courtenay, and Alan Bates all found fame on Broadway, and were offered Hollywood contracts, but they wanted to do theater work, and returned to Britain. They were fortunate enough to get their start when these new playwrights were beginning.

British playwrights were lucky enough to have very well-known actors in their plays. Alan Bates and Simon Gray worked well together. Tom Courtenay and Albert Finney had a marvelous success in Ronald Harwood's play *The Dresser*, and Alan Bennett could get almost any British star to act in his plays. David Hare, who is the most produced living playwright at the National Theatre, first started writing in the 1960s. *Plenty* proved one of the most successful exports to Broadway, winning rave reviews and the New York Critics Circle Award.

In the early 1970s, PBS television started showing *Upstairs Downstairs* and *Brideshead Revisited*, and among the American public there was a terrific surge of interest in British drama. Jean Marsh and Eileen Atkins, who created *Upstairs Downstairs*, became household names— and still are—as the series is still airing in many parts of the U.S.

Eileen Atkins had been to the States already, and starred in *The Killing of Sister George* in 1967, but she said even at that time that unless a theater actress does TV work in Britain you cannot make ends meet. All you do is subsidize the theater when you work in London, as the salaries are so low. She told a reporter that she felt more glamorous in America, and she was very tempted to stay there. She said there is always a chance there of doing a Shakespeare play for people who don't know how it ends. Along with Rosemary Harris, Zoë Caldwell, and Zoë Wanamaker, she gets much of her best work done in New York.

She continued that when she comes home and waits for the next job, it nearly always comes from

America. In England, whenever you play a part they all remember how Sybil Thorndike or Edith Evans or Irene Worth used to do it; in America you can say, look, forget everything you know about this play, if anything, start here and now with me. In England you can never get critics or audiences to do that. She knows that there is a danger of ending up in mid-Atlantic if you try to plan a career in both countries, but it just seems to happen that the best offers come from the U.S.: "The English are good with words, they're brilliant technicians, but Americans act with guts, so both nationalities benefit from working together."

Eileen Atkins first met Vanessa Redgrave in Stratford in 1955, and they have been close friends ever since. Both Vanessa and Lynn have had successes on Broadway, followed by the younger Redgrave generation, and in the 1990s Eileen Atkins devised a play called *Vita and Virginia* from the letters of Vita Sackville West and Virginia Woolf which was a great hit in New York, starring Vanessa and Eileen, with Zoë Caldwell directing. In 2003 Eileen returned to Broadway to star in a play called *Return to Moscow* with John Lithgow.

Pauline Collins, another actress who appeared in *Upstairs Downstairs*, was a great success in *Shirley Valentine* on Broadway, and people wanted to see these British actors in the theater. Jeremy Irons, after his appearance in *Brideshead Revisited*, starred in *The Real Thing*, and was almost an overnight success in becoming a face-recognizable actor when he began his career in feature films. It is ironic to think that all these theater actors were now finding success in the United States through the exposure of their work in British television.

Judi Dench said she had been acting for years on stage, but it wasn't till after she had done a TV show that people started recognizing her in the street. Her TV series *As Time Goes by* is now shown regularly on PBS across America.

When Dame Judi Dench went to New York to appear on Broadway in David Hare's play *Amy's View* in 1999, there was a dinner party to welcome her at the French restaurant Chez Josephine (see Chapter 1) on West 42nd Street, which is owned by one of Josephine Baker's adopted sons, John Claude Baker.

During the run of the play Dame Judi was presented with the Sir John Gielgud Award for Excellence in the Dramatic Arts by the Shakespeare Guild, at the Barrymore Theater in New York. The award itself was the Golden Quill. Judi told her biographer John Miller: "They're keeping me in the dark about what's actually going to happen. I think it's scenes from Shakespeare, and I believe Richard Eyre and David Hare are doing a cabaret act."

Christopher Plummer began the evening's tribute.

I was lucky enough to be in the same company as Judi Dench, the Royal Shakespeare Company in London and Stratford-upon-Avon. What a formidable company it was that year. Not only were the senior alumni represented by John Gielgud and Dame Peggy Ashcroft, but each one of the leading younger members of the company became a star in his or her own right. A young Sir Peter Hall, a young Franco Zeffirelli, a young Colin Blakeley, Ian Bannen, Christopher Plummer—what a cast! And the leading ladies— a hilarious Geraldine McEwan, a magical Dorothy Tutin, a wondrously young Vanessa Redgrave and, youngest of all, a pert, delectable, talented, enchanting Judi Dench.

She was already in tears by the time he ended with a poem to her and was relieved when the auditorium was darkened for the screening of two scenes from *Mrs. Brown*. Hal Holbrook followed with a speech by Shylock, happily unaware that it was from Judi's least favorite Shakespeare play. Richard Eyre spoke of how the one quality Judi has never seemed to need is luck, "but for we mortals who need it badly, and who have become her friends, and who have worked with her, she has been part of our luck."

After the tribute was over Dame Judi crossed the road to have dinner at the Supper Club. On arrival she stood and shook hands with over two hundred people who wanted to congratulate her, while her well-earned dinner turned cold on the table behind her. The receiving line kept up for over an hour and she delighted everybody. In his biography of Judi, John Miller tells of her total dedication to the production she is working on. The Supper Club is a large venue with a cabaret room upstairs where well-known artists appear. That night it was closed for the private party.

Judi has her regular routine when working in a play. She is usually one of the first of the actors to arrive at the theater. She has the cup of tea with honey in it, and later on she takes a little phial of ginseng and royal jelly. She says it's just like drinking pure honey, and she takes it before each performance, matinée and evening. "I wouldn't feel right if I didn't have that." The energy needed to get through a long part is enormous, and she used to go out for tea between a matinée and an evening show, but during the run of *Amy's View* on Broadway, she found that she needed to sleep instead. During that run at the Barrymore, the crew would grill a barbecue lunch every Sunday in the back lot behind the theater, and the cast would bring contributions to the buffet.

In 1999 she was the first actress to win both an Oscar and a Tony in the same year since Ellen Burstyn twenty years before. But as Miller writes, "Awards matter less to Judi than parts." Just before she left for America she received an invitation from Trevor Nunn to return to the National Theatre in a particular play that lacked appeal for her. She replied, "I want to come back to the National, but not in that part. Would you ask me to do something more frightening than that?"

There can be little doubt that he will, nor that Peter Hall, Richard Eyre, and many others will not be far behind. She will certainly make more films—the offers are now pouring in—and she will continue to appear on television and radio, but we can rest assured that she will not deny us the chance to see and hear her in her natural habitat— the stage.

Michael Crawford, Jim Dale, and Robert Lindsay were rediscovered in the U.S., and in 1981 Sir Ian McKellen said on his return from playing Salieri in *Amadeus*: "I can't convey what a hit on Broadway is like. It's overwhelming." He recalls the night when he received his Tony award for the role. "I came out of the building and a huge scream went up. I looked around to see who they were screaming at, and it was for me." Jane Lapotaire was also there that night receiving her Tony for her brilliant performance as Piaf in Peter Hall's production.

Diana Rigg went on a six-month tour in 1974 in the National Theatre's modern version of Moliere's *The Misanthrope*, which was directed by John Dexter, but she didn't become a celebrity in the U.S. until the TV series *The Avengers* was shown.

Many actors have their "comfort" food, although the term is little known in the States. Judi Dench has her tea with honey in it, and I asked David Suchet when he was on Broadway playing Salieri in *Amadeus* what his was: "Corned beef hash with a fried egg on top." "Something eggy on toast on a tray" was what Noël Coward liked when he was confined to bed with a cold or exhaustion.

Peter Hall, Richard Eyre, Michael Blakemore, John Dexter, and most of the younger directors at the National and RSC have all worked on Broadway. However there are some American directors who want to work with British actors in New York, and one of the most brilliant of these is Mike Nichols. He has the knack of putting his own spin on a British play, and he has helped to enlarge the reputation of many British performers and playwrights on Broadway. Nichols has since gone on to direct feature films but he got his start in the theater when he worked with Elaine May in revue and cabaret work.

Two directors who were working regularly in New York during the 1970s and '80s were Peter Hall and John Dexter. Sir Peter still does. In his *Diaries*, first published in 1983, he has many accounts of his productions not only on Broadway but with the Metropolitan Opera Company as well. He juggled new productions on both sides of the Atlantic, between endless meetings and rehearsal schedules, as he was Artistic Director of the National Theatre up till 1988. Sir Peter seems to possess more energy than any other director on either side of the Atlantic. When Alan Ayckbourn's play *Bedroom Farce* transferred to Broadway, American Equity demanded that the British cast be replaced after twelve weeks by an American cast, so Sir Peter had to fly over to audition the U.S.

actors, He wrote that the American actors treated him like God. "But the very English idiom of Ayckbourn's play really is almost impossible for them. I feel as if I am encouraging them to wear funny hats." In his autobiography he says that rehearsing with talented actors in something he likes to do every day: "It is up to me to hold their interest, to inspire them, and I must give unsparingly of my energy. It is almost an erotic passion."

John Dexter hated working at the National and preferred to remain in New York. He went to New York after his early career at the Royal Court Theatre with George Devine where he directed Arnold Wesker's first plays, including *Roots*. It was in this play that Joan Plowright became an overnight success. Dexter continued to direct both in the West End and for Laurence Olivier at the National until he left for New York in 1974. He became the Director of Productions at the Metropolitan Opera as well as directing plays on Broadway including Richard Burton in Peter Shaffer's *Equus*.

Anthony Hopkins first played the role of the psychiatrist in *Equus* on Broadway in the mid-1970s, supported by a strong cast that included Peter Firth, Marion Seldes, Frances Sternhagen, Michael Higgins, and as the stablegirl, Roberta Maxwell. Dennis Brown in his book *Actors Talk* writes about interviewing Roberta during the run of the show. "Our director, John Dexter, can be a very difficult man," she said with a laugh.

He's one of Guthrie's boys, a pint-sized Guthrie, a real weasely version of Dr. Guthrie. [More seriously] There's one thing on his mind at all times, and that is the work. The work is everything. He instilled in us that we must not be complacent, that you are only as good as the ground you stand on, and that everything else except the work is absolutely irrelevant to an artist.

First he broke us down physically. We did rigorous physical exercise for half an hour before every rehearsal. Then when we were literally prone and exhausted on the floor, lying on our stomachs gasping for air, one of us would get up and read his or her favorite poem. Through those poems, we found out a lot about each other. Within two days we were a functioning company, all working for the same thing, which was the play.

After that first preview Dexter pulled us back. We were all on tenterhooks, and Dexter kept us like horses reined in. Never gave us anything. "Well, darlings, now you've done that, you think you've accomplished something. Well, it's just not so. You've got a million miles to go." So we were kept going and going right up to the last day.

On the last day he did something incredible. He said, "Right, darlings, you're all coming in in the afternoon. We're going to watch the understudies do the show." Our hearts fell. Nobody wanted to do it. The understudies didn't want to do it. We all wanted to kill him. He said, "And we'll have a little drink before they perform."

We came at 12 o'clock, and he had a sumptuous feast laid on in the downstairs foyer. Cold salmon, lox, French champagne. We all got quite merry. Then we went upstairs, and the understudies did the first act. During the break Dexter said, "Now darlings, we don't want to see any more of that. Everybody go up onstage and you'll all do a poem for me." So we did poems, and by that time we were no longer high. We all had headaches, but it was too late to go home and take a bath. So we went to our dressing rooms. We opened our packages and telegrams. We all loved each other. Such a unit. Such care. And it was him. Incredible man. Work, work. Beyond and above everything. Manipulative emotionally. John Dexter had driven us to a peak for that one moment, opening night. And then we came onstage and did the play.

At the end, there was a tremendous ovation. And Peter Shaffer's face shone, because he'd been afraid. We were all afraid how the play would be perceived. Afterwards there was a huge party. Dexter wouldn't come. He was left on the corner with a torn paper bag trying to get a taxi. Looked miserable. His job was finished.

Separation is the name of the game when a play is taken over to Broadway. Show business marriages have to be extremely strong to survive if one partner is working on Broadway and the other is left at home working in a play or tied up with other issues such as children at school or domestic problems.

When Billie Whitelaw went over to play in Samuel Beckett's plays, she was a smash hit. Staying at the Algonquin Hotel, she missed her family desperately. The newspapers, radio, and media were clamoring for her, but she said she just wanted to get on with the show and go home. She found the hectic and frantic publicity round-about quite amazing. It was a sensational success, but the exposure was not something to become addicted to, which many stars welcomed and came to expect. After first arriving in New York, unpacking and then going down to the theater she found that she had no dressing room, and that the theater was still being built.

Julie Andrews, Rex Harrison, and Richard and Sybil Burton all had problems of family separations, and often actors' careers have been totally changed because of this. Not only did marriages suffer, but when Jessie Matthews went over to New York in Charles Cochran's *Revue of 1924*, she went almost as a child. She was wined and dined when touring and during the New York run, so that when she returned to London in sophisticated clothes, in place of the young schoolgirl there was an elegant sophisticated young woman in silk hose, high heels, and make-up. As Michael Thornton recounts in his biography, her parents blinked in disbelief. "What's the matter with you?" said her mother. Jessie felt as if she had been slapped in the face. "I suppose we're not good enough for you now," remarked her father.

It is interesting to note the New York audiences often come to expect that British stars who come to Broadway should appear in historical plays, if not Shakespeare then something that meets their expectation of a classic British play. Often they are rewarded. Paul Scofield made his New York debut in Robert Bolt's *A Man for All Seasons* in 1961 as Sir Thomas More, Geraldine McEwan in 1963 playing Lady Teazle in Sheridan's *School for Scandal*, and so the list goes on. Derek Jacobi, already known from his TV series *I Claudius*, played in Erdmann's *The Suicide* and Glenda Jackson's debut was in *Marat/Sade* directed by Peter Brook. She later played the lead in the RSC's production of Ibsen's *Hedda Gabler* on Broadway.

Among the most recent companies have been Cheek by Jowl, the Royal Shakespeare Company, the Almeida Theatre's production of *Medea* with Diana Rigg and Ralph Fiennes' *Hamlet*. In 1998 Richard Eyre directed Liam Neeson in David Hare's play *The Judas Kiss*.

Many of these actors stayed at the Algonquin Hotel which is a short walk from Broadway, and they were staying in surroundings very much like home. The cuisine used to include all the comfort foods, like rice pudding and steak and kidney pie—meals from an Agatha Christie novel.

Broadway has seen its fair share of successful impresarios down the years. The most famous still remains Florenz Ziegfeld, whose showgirls and spectacular scenery still define an age of glamor for us, some sixty years after his heyday. Yet of all the well-heeled cigar-chomping men who have left their mark on the Great White Way, the most successful, and still the most influential, after some fifteen years at the top, is a Scotsman named Cameron Mackintosh. Yet, although he is undeniably British, and proud of it, the richest showman of the century has a life story that reads like a piece of the American Dream.

Born in 1946 into a comfortably-off family, he decided as a child that he was going to have a career in the theater. Not as an actor, singer, or dancer, or any of the obviously attractive, public sides of show business, but as a producer. And not just a producer, but a producer of musicals.

This ambition came to him when he was eight years old (as he proudly recounts in his *Who's Who* entry). The show that sparked this desire was *Salad Days*, Julian Slade's charming musical about a magic piano and a young couple in love, that was one of the hits of the London stage in the early 1950s. The show was revived in the late 1990s, at the Vaudeville Theatre, in a production that was directed by Ned Sherrin, the theater historian, director, raconteur, and wit. Cameron Mackintosh turned up at the first night in full Highland gear, including a kilt!

The impresario-to-be began his theater career as a student at the Central School of Speech and Drama, but dropped out to get some practical experience—a much more American than British thing to do.

He started as a stagehand at the Theatre Royal, Drury Lane. Although the job was a menial one, it at least meant that he was, at an early age, earning a living—however meager—in show business. And where better to start than Drury Lane, the home of so many great British musicals, from Noël Coward's *Cavalcade*, through the extraordinary run of Ivor Novello hits in the 1930s—*Glamorous Night*, *Careless Rapture*, *Crest of the Wave*, and, of course, *The Dancing Years*? Later it had been the home of *My Fair Lady*, and little did the actresses who noticed the young stagehand with the big brown eyes realize that one day he would break box-office records as producer of a show—*Miss Saigon*.

The run of shows that was to make him one of the richest men in the world (with an estimated fortune of some three-quarters of a billion dollars), and which was celebrated by an extraordinary, star-studded tribute to him at the Lyceum Theatre in London's West End (*Hey Mr. Producer*, 1998) began in a relatively low key, with *Little Women* in 1967, but in 1969 he tried his first London musical, *Anything Goes*.

He experimented with many shows, suffering the usual slings and arrows that fortune throws at producers, but Mackintosh was convinced that he would, indeed, make his fortune. The theme of this book has been the close connection between the English and American stage, and it was, appropriately, through an American composer that Sir Cameron (he was knighted by the Queen in 1996) made his mark. This was through his production of *Side by Side* by Steven Sondheim, in 1976.

Sondheim has long been a very popular composer and lyricist in England, a fact attested both by the number of commercial productions of his work mounted in the West End over the years, and by the fondness for his work that the National Theatre has demonstrated, with critically acclaimed performances, for example, of *Sweeney Todd* and, in 1995, with Dame Judi Dench and the marvelous Sian Phillips (ex-wife of Peter O'Toole), of *A Little Night Music.*

Sir Cameron returned to his British roots almost immediately, however, putting his Sondheim profits into a production of Lionel Bart's *Oliver!*, a show that he revived, in a new version, at the London Palladium in 1994. One of the several stars to play Fagin was Jonathan Pryce; another was Jim Dale. Dale, initially famous as a member of the *Carry On* team (the *Carry On* series being an enormously popular series of film comedies from the late 1950s to the mid-1970s, and at its heyday in the 1960s), went on to a very distinguished stage career in America, yet another on the long roll-call of British acting talent that, despite success at home, has found a niche in New York.

By 1994, Lionel Bart had long since sold his rights to the show, but Sir Cameron insisted not only on bringing him into the production at a very early stage, but gave him a cut of the profits too. This is a typical gesture of his, characterized in two ways. First, he is a generous man who has given a great deal of money to charity, particularly that associated with theater. Secondly, having had so much fun as well as having made so much money from the business, he is a strong believer in putting something back in. This takes the form not just of employing, directly and indirectly, huge numbers of people in productions all over the world, but in conserving Britain's theatrical heritage, and reminding the young of it existence.

Two examples of this will have to suffice: first, that he brought much of the memorabilia and theater collections to the Theatre Museum; second, that he has endowed a professorship of contemporary theater at Oxford University, so that the giants of the West End stage can share their experience with a new generation of actors, designers—and, of course, impresarios. One of the greatest living British impresarios, Michael Codron, was one of the first people to be honored by this one-year-long appointment.

Although Sir Cameron continued to produce tried and tested shows like *My Fair Lady* and *Oklahoma!*, it was a new and in many ways apparently foolhardy venture that raised him from comfortable success to fame and enormous wealth. The show was *Cats*, the year was 1981, the composer was Andrew Lloyd Webber (later Sir Andrew, now Lord Lloyd Webber).

Lloyd Webber, with his lyricist Tim Rice, had successes with *Joseph and his Amazing Technicolor Dream Coat*, and *Jesus Christ Superstar*. Turning a collection of T.S. Eliot's poems about cats into a major West End musical was another matter altogether, and Lloyd Webber was risking his bank balance as well as his reputation on the show—as was Mackintosh.

Sir Cameron's rise seemed unstoppable once he teamed up with Lloyd Webber. After producing *Song and Dance* in 1982, he went his own way, with *Blondel* (lyricist Tim Rice) and *Little Shop of Horrors*, the latter demonstrating his affection for (and shrewd judgment over) quirky small-scale shows that nonetheless had great popular appeal. His affection for British composers, as well as shows that reflected a nostalgia for bygone days, was demonstrated by his backing a production of Sandy Wilson's wonderful tribute to the 1920s, *The Boyfriend*, in 1984.

The mid-1980s were to see Sir Cameron's next big success with *Les Miserables*, directed by Trevor Nunn. Still running at the Palace Theatre (owned by Lord Lloyd Webber's company, the entertainingly named Really Useful Group), *Les Miserables* was an international sensation. Its success is a tribute to Sir Cameron's judgment, but the run of the musical in New York has also demonstrated the ruthlessness that is a vital ingredient for success in the theater—or in any business, for that matter.

After the show had been running for many years on Broadway, he decided that it was getting a little tired, and that new blood was needed. Some of the French revolutionary students had been in the production for years, and he decided to replace them with new actors. This caused a storm of protest from the cast members who had been given their marching orders, but Sir Cameron stood firm, and public opinion seemed to side with him. Several references were made to the fact that the *Miserables* students were beginning to look rather mature for their roles. Whatever the rights or wrongs of individual cases, he was surely right in principle, in that there is no such thing as a guaranteed long-term job in the theater—or in any business, for that matter. Even the longest running show in the world, Agatha Christie's *The Mousetrap* (originally at the Ambassador's Theatre, now at the neighboring St. Martin's) has a complete cast change once a year to keep the play (first produced in 1952) fresh!

The second generation of theatrical families are now making their own impact in New York and their proud parents come to applaud them when not working in the theater themselves. Amanda Plummer starred in *Agnes of God* during the 1990s in New York and her father Christopher Plummer will star in *King Lear* in 2004. She is the daughter of the actress Tammy Grimes, who has starred on Broadway many times. Richard Burton's daughter, Kate, is following in her father's footsteps and there is too, of course, the young generation of Redgraves.

In 2000 Jennifer Ehle made her Broadway debut in the British play, *The Real Thing*, and won a Tony Award as Best Actress for her performance. Interestingly her mother, Rosemary Harris, was also nominated for the Best Actress Award that year and even though they were in competition with each other Rosemary was thrilled when her daughter won. Jennifer next starred in Noël Coward's *Design for Living* with co-stars Alan Cumming and Dominic West.

This younger generation have found their own restaurants to dine in after the show. The French restaurant, Café Un, Deux, Trois, on West 44th Street is very popular and has the atmosphere or rather ambience of La Coupole in Paris—with almost the same menu and the same terracotta tiled floors. Another popular place on West 44th Street is Angus McIndoe. Angus greets you at the door with his thick Scottish accent and with a charming smile. The place is quite small compared to Sardi's just up the street, but he is host to the many actors who descend through his doors after their performances on Broadway.

Three Walks through New York's Theaterland

Between Sixth and Eighth Avenues, which run north and south, you find that theaterland starts on the cross-streets beginning at 42nd Street and continuing up to 54th Street. Broadway cuts across the middle. You can walk from Broadway down each street from 42nd to 54th, and find all the most prestigious theaters just off Times Square. However, let's begin with the most famous hotels and restaurants.

WALK ONE: THEATERLAND

Besides the actual theaters of Broadway, there are many dramatic and colorful venues in New York which attract British performers when staying in New York. Their New York counterparts would entertain them, wine and dine them in these glamorous hotels and restaurants. Their friends were writers, painters, musicians, as well as theater people, people such as Scott Fitzgerald, Dorothy Parker, Kay Thompson, Neysa McMein, and the Lunts. On this walk you will visit some of these places which are still as popular today as they were fifty years ago.

Start at the Plaza Hotel on Fifth Avenue at 59th Street. Walk through the main lobby to see the renowned Palm Court. It is located amid a profusion of greenery in the heart of the Plaza Hotel's lobby, long recognized as one of the premier meeting places in New York and an enchanting European café at the hub of the Plaza lifestyle. Filled with serenades of piano at lunch and piano and violin from afternoon tea until late evening, the Palm Court is a lively indoor café that hums with activity from early breakfast to après-theater dining. It is reminiscent of an outdoor English café where people-watching is a beloved pastime.

This was the same Tea Court sacred to the memory of the elegant Edwardians, later the popular haunt of the 1930s as the Palm Court, and still later, the luncheon setting for calorie-conscious ladies who nibbled on salads; the place where, as *New York Times* society editor Russell Edward wrote, "Nobody raises an eyebrow if you order tea at cocktail time."

A 1907 guest would be right at home in today's Palm Court, which the builders then called The Lounge and guests called The Tea Room. It was modeled on the lines of the wonderful Winter Garden in London's Carlton Hotel, but with special touches all its own. The domed ceiling was executed in pastel green and yellow leaded glass for the hotel by Louis Comfort Tiffany, but was removed in 1944 as part of Conrad Hilton's renovations. The French-style mirrored rear wall accented arches supported by four marble caryatids, representing the four seasons. Columns and tabletops were made of fleur de peche marble, and today, sixty to sixty-five tables are said to be original.

A few days after the hotel opened on October 1, 1907, they looked down upon young Gladys Vanderbilt, who lived in her father's house across the street, sitting in the Tea Room with Count Laslo Szechenyi, saying "yes" to his offer of marriage. It was the beginning of still another tradition, courting at The Plaza.

The British actress, Mrs. Patrick Campbell, arrived at The Plaza from England on November 8, 1907, for the theatrical engagement *Hedda Gabler*. Traveling with her seventeen-year-old and blind monkey-spitz poodle, one week later on November 15, she lights a cigarette in the Palm Court, making herself the first woman in America to smoke a cigarette in a public place. Her response to management was, "My dear fellow, I have been given to understand this is a free country. I intend to do nothing to alter its status." One result of her bravado was that smoking was banned on subways two years later.

Over the years, a lot of less-than-romantic people have tried to change the Tea Room into something different. But, fortunately for romance, the room isn't much different today than it was in the beginning. The Tiffany ceiling is gone, unfortunately, victim to the removal of the open courtyard above it, and the name has been changed. They began calling it the Palm Court in the mid-1930s.

Kay Thompson used to stay with Coward at his home in England and Switzerland; they used to play two-piano duets together, and she was always included when he entertained. Kay was a gifted singer, writer, arranger, made her Broadway debut in 1937, and also had a successful cabaret act which was performed at London's Café de Paris. Her one-woman show ran on Broadway in 1954.

On the other side of the Palm Court is the Oak Room, where a plaque to George M. Cohan (Mr. Broadway) can be seen in the far right-hand corner above the booth where he always sat, plotting Broadway shows and doing business. He wrote the famous song "Give my Regards to Broadway." Don't miss the Edwardian elegance of the murals in the Oyster Bar.

F. Scott Fitzgerald and his wife Zelda were, for a time, residents. They loved the hotel. Ernest Hemingway once advised Fitzgerald to donate his liver to Princeton and give his heart to the Plaza.

Cross Fifth Avenue and go south to East 55th Street, and turn left to the St. Regis Hotel. This is where the Oliviers stayed. The mural in the King Cole Room was painted by Maxwell Parrish, and used to be on the wall in Rector's, the celebrated restaurant on Broadway, before it closed many years ago. Take the elevator up to the roof to view the lovely ballroom. The most lavish balls and parties were held here for the Windsors, and after first nights. They still are! Ivor Novello and Noël Coward partied here.

Continuing along East 55th Street to Park Avenue, turn south to the Waldorf Hotel at 50th Street. It is here, in the Waldorf Towers, that the Windsors lived when they were in New York, in the residential part of the hotel. Cole Porter lived there too for over twenty-five years. His piano used to be in Peacock Alley, off the main lobby, but it has now been moved to the Terrace Room above the foyer. Pianists still play it for afternoon teas and the cocktail hour. Somerset Maugham, Winston Churchill, Elizabeth Taylor, Marilyn Monroe, Ava Gardner, Grace Kelly, and Prince Rainier have all stayed at the hotel, and it is still full of the atmosphere of that gilded jazz age of the 1920s.

Walk across along 49th Street back towards Fifth Avenue and you will come to the famed Rockefeller Center. Walk through the building, to see the Art Deco sculptures on the walls both inside and outside, the outdoor skating rink, and then take the express elevator up to the top of the building to see the view from Rainbow Room (see Chapter 1).

Back down again, exit on Sixth Avenue, and walk down 45th Street one block west across to Times Square, to the Half Price ticket booth perhaps, for tickets for that evening's show; if you can face another elevator, go across to the Marriott

Hotel on Times Square and take one of their glass elevators up to the revolving bar and restaurant, which overlook theaterland and Times Square, for a drink or dinner.

WALK TWO:
FROM A PICNIC TO A FEAST IN CENTRAL PARK

Start at the Boathouse Restaurant in Central Park which is situated in the middle of the Park between West 72nd Street and on the East Side at Fifth Avenue. In fact there is a trolleycar in the summer months which takes you from the Fifth Avenue entrance to the pretty Boathouse right on the lake. In the summer the view from this elegant restaurant across the lake is a pure joy, and the cuisine at the cafe includes modern American dishes with plenty of exotic salads and fish. As you dine you can watch the rowboats bobbing by, which are for rent nearby, and also a gondola which was imported from Italy for rides on the lake. However, the gondolier doesn't sing.

From here walk up through the Ramble, a wooded area, well sign-posted to the Belvedere Castle. On your right you will pass Shakespeare's Garden where many of the plants and herbs are mentioned in Shakespeare's plays. Further on you will come to the Delacorte Theater where you can watch Shakespeare in the open air. One of the favorite summer pastimes of New Yorkers is a picnic in Central Park, and many theater-goers bring a picnic before attending a performance. The Delacorte is open-air, similar to the open-air theatre in London's Regents Park. Producer and director Joseph Papp organized the New York Shakespeare Festival in 1954 and began giving free performances in Central Park on a temporary stage in 1957. In 1962, publisher George Delacorte Jr. built the Delacorte Theater at the edge of the Great Lawn as a permanent stage for the festival.

Returning south, the walk returns back to the West 72nd entrance to the park. One block further south is the entrance to the "Tavern on the Green," the most famous theater restaurant in the park. There is a large garden dining area as well as the famous Crystal Room where some Broadway first night parties are held.

During the day the ornate Chinese lanterns, elaborate plants, and flowering trees create a lovely atmosphere; in the evening hundreds of tiny lights thread through the trees and around the gardens. The restaurant holds many private functions as well in its several smaller dining rooms. On one such occasion Dame Judi Dench and Vanessa Redgrave were honored with awards by the Women's Project, an organization which funds and promotes women in the theater.

The walk continues back along West 72nd Street and down Broadway to see the famous "Wedding Cake" building at 2109 Broadway called The Ansonia. Because of its ornate beaux arts style, the building acquired this nickname and the plaque over the front door names some of the former residents. Enrico Caruso, Toscanini, and Florenz Ziegfeld of the Ziegfeld Follies all lived here, and it is almost as famous as the Dakota apartments on the corner of West 72nd Street and Central Park West.

When actors moved out of the hotels featured in Chapter 1, their next step would be an apartment, so it is interesting to follow through to find out where they lived after leaving these hotels.

Cross Broadway to West 67th Street and perhaps end your walk with a drink or dinner at the Café des Artistes on the left-hand side of the street just before you reach Central Park West.

WALK THREE:
DOWN MEMORY LANE

Starting at West 44th Street just west of Broadway, you will find Sardi's restaurant on your left with the Helen Hayes Theater next door. Helen Hayes was often called the "First Lady of the American Theater." She was a stage star for over fifty years, retiring in 1971. With a long list of leading roles, she had a great success playing *Mary of Scotland* (1933) and *Victoria Regina* (1935). Lynn Redgrave starred in her own show *Shakespeare for my Father* at this theater. Opposite is the Shubert Theater next to Shubert Alley. The history of the Shubert Organization, their theaters alone, would fill a book, but it is interesting to stand outside the entrance knowing you are in the heart of theaterland. The Shubert brothers are legendary; the Shubert Organization currently manages sixteen theaters on Broadway. The heartbeat of the firm is upstairs in offices over this theater.

Walk further down the street to see the St. James's Theater on your left. It opened in 1927 with a George M. Cohan musical. It was here that *Oklahoma!* (five-year run) and *The King and I*—starring Gertie Lawrence in her last stage appearance—had long runs. Originally named the Erlanger Theater it has 1,600 seats. Highlights of the 1960s included Laurence Olivier in *Beckett*, Albert Finney in *Luther*. More recent productions include Jim Dale in *Barnum* and Twiggy in *My One and Only*. Cross the street to the celebrated Majestic Theater. It was here that *Camelot* opened in 1960 with Richard Burton and Julie Andrews, and in 1988, *Phantom of the Opera*. Because of its large seating capacity, musicals have been frequently moved here when they become hits, as did *42nd Street*.

Walking up Broadway, you will come into Times Square and you will see Planet Hollywood with all its neon lights inviting you to enter. Bruce Willis and other Hollywood stars are often seen dining here as it is still a place to rub shoulders with celebrities. Times Square has many fast food places including pizza and hamburger take-outs as well as hot dog stands.

Carmen's Restaurant just off Broadway on West 45th Street features Italian food and is very popular with resident New Yorkers as well as tourists.

Cross Broadway at 45th Street, to find the Lyceum Theater a short distance along on the other side of Broadway. If possible try to see the historic penthouse apartment of the theater which is the home of the Shubert Archive, but once was the apartment of Daniel Frohman, the original owner/producer. He lived there with his wife, the actress Margaret Illington, and the peephole in the apartment which was made so he could watch her performances is still there. They would entertain there and give after-theater parties for the cast. It is the oldest Broadway theater still in operation, and was declared a landmark in 1975. Two British plays which were hits in the 1960s were *A Taste of Honey* by Shelagh Delaney, starring Angela Lansbury and Joan Plowright (who won a Tony award), and Harold Pinter's *The Caretaker*, starring Alan Bates, Robert Shaw, and Donald Pleasance. Later came John Osborne's *Look Back in Anger*. Across the street is the original Stanford White building which used to house the famous Lambs Club. It is now a church.

Walking back down 45th Street you will find the Music Box Theater—look for the historic plaque in the lobby in honor of Irving Berlin. The Music Box was named by Berlin, and he was half-owner with the Shubert Organization until his death. His musical *Of Thee I Sing* became the first musical to win the Pulitzer Prize. Further on is the Martin Beck Theater at 302 West 45th Street, where the Abbey Players (from Dublin) and the D'Oyly Carte

Company played. The 1,300-seat theater was named after a leading vaudeville producer of the 1920s. Also on West 45th Street is the Plymouth Theater, built in 1917 by Arthur Hopkins as a theatrical home for himself and his productions. The RSC's production of *Nicholas Nickleby* ran for eight hours with a dinner break. Tickets were $100, a record price in 1981. Leslie Howard played Hamlet here in 1936.

As you cross Times Square you can see the statue of "Mr. Broadway," George M. Cohan, on the pedestrian island in the middle of the street. As a rest from looking at theaters, walk down Restaurant Row on West 46th Street between Seventh and Ninth Avenues. Joe Allen's is on the left, Don't Tell Mama on your right, and a dozen other theater restaurants that will offer you a pre-theater dinner. Joe Allen's is the most famous with the theatrical profession. Don't Tell Mama has a cabaret room where showcases are held for new talent as well as regular shows with well-known performers. Many songwriters try out material here with favorite performers singing their works. Cabaret is more popular in New York than in London, it seems, with many more rooms to hear musical revues and performers.

Walking back along West 47th Street from Eighth Avenue towards Broadway, the Brooks Atkinson Theater is on your right. It is named after the eminent drama critic of the *New York Times*. Tallulah Bankhead made her final appearance here. In 1990 Nigel Hawthorne won a New York Tony Award for his performance in *Shadowlands*, the British play about C.S. Lewis. In the 1980s Rex Harrison, Claudette Colbert, and Lynn Redgrave starred in Frederic Lonsdale's play *Aren't We All*. British actors who have played here are Albert Finney, Zena Walker, Tom Courtenay, and Paul Rogers, among many others.

Across the street is the Ethel Barrymore Theater. This beautiful theater was built by the Shuberts in honor of the beloved Ethel Barrymore and opened on December 20, 1928, with the actress starring in *The Kingdom of God*.

In the 1930s Fred Astaire made his last Broadway appearance here in Cole Porter's *Gay Divorce*, and Katharine Cornell and Laurence Olivier appeared in *No Time for Comedy*. It is where Maggie Smith, Michael Redgrave, and Michael Crawford too have played. Orson Welles' production of *Moby Dick* with Rod Steiger was first presented here.

Walk up Broadway to West 55th Street, and turn left to the Hotel Edison to relax in the Art Deco lobby.

EPILOGUE

Food for the Spirit

P.G. Wodehouse was married to Ethel Newton in the Little Church Around the Corner at 1 East 29th Street (known as the Church of the Transfiguration) in 1914. There is a memorial plaque dedicated to him in the church. On the plaque is a quote from him: "The only church that anybody could be married at. It's on 29th Street, just around the corner from Fifth Avenue. It's got a fountain playing in front of it and it's a little bit of Heaven dumped right down in the middle of New York." Immediately underneath his plaque is another one dedicated to Walter Edmund Bentley who was an actor-priest and founder of the Actors' Church Alliance which was a charity for actors to see that they always had a hot meal when unemployed. To the right of these plaques, two feet away, is one for Rex Harrison whose memorial service was held here.

The quaint name is supposed to derive from an incident in 1870 when Joseph Jefferson was having great difficulty in finding a church which would allow the funeral of an actor friend of his. Finally a colleague told him that "there is a little church around the corner where they do that sort of thing," i.e. bury actors. Since that time theater people have felt a special affection for the little church. Edwin Booth's funeral was held here in 1893.

Historically, the Church of the Transfiguration started life in 1848 in a private house on East 24th Street, until it found its permanent home a year later when the construction of the present building was completed. The first rector, George Hendric Houghton, initiated in the Episcopalian Church in the United States the Oxford Movement which had originated in England. This movement was founded on the desire to make the services of the Anglican and related churches closer to those of the Roman Catholic church. During his ministry at the Little Church Around the Corner, George Houghton also sheltered escaped slaves from the South during the Civil War, and provided food for the destitute.

It also saw, in 1923, the birth of the Episcopal Actors' Guild of America, which was intended to foster two-way communication between theater people and the Episcopal church.

The first president of the Episcopal Actors' Guild was George Arliss. Other well-known names served as presidents or officers of the Guild, including such luminaries as Rex Harrison, Tallulah Bankhead, Cornelia Otis Skinner, Charlton Heston, Joan Fontaine, and many others. The romantic and theatrical associations of the church make it popular, not merely to actors, as the setting for marriages, baptisms, or simply as a place to worship.

Another church that has theatrical associations is St. Malachy's on West 43rd Street. "We have a show running for the last hundred years," said Father Kelly, vicar of St. Malachy's, known as the actors' chapel. The equivalent in London would be St. Paul's, known as the actors' church in Covent Garden, and like St. Malachy's located in the heart of theaterland. It is ironic that in medieval times actors were not allowed to be buried in consecrated ground because their profession was regarded as sinful.

St. Malachy's first opened in 1903 and celebrated its centennial with its own street sign. Spencer Tracy and Bob Hope were regulars and Douglas Fairbanks married Joan Crawford there, Rudolph Valentino's funeral in 1926 was held there and thousands lined the streets to watch the procession. Melanie Griffiths, Rosalind Russell, and Brian Dennehy have also lit candles at the church.

Historically it has always been a refuge for actors and in the 1920s the church was open for midnight mass, mainly for actors who wanted to go there after the theater. Most of the masses today are held during the day. But there is a story of how famous the church became when in 1944 it was selected as the church in the film *Going My Way*, which starred Bing Crosby. Even now, Father Kelly with his Irish accent has been cast in films. In the 1996 movie *City Hall*, starring Al Pacino, Father

Kelly played a priest, although he said "Instead of giving the last rites I think I baptized them."

So, from Broadway, its theaters, restaurants, theatrical clubs and all the special people who made it, and continue to make it, the magical place it is, we have attempted to capture some of the magic.

This book celebrates the past but looks forward to the future. We are confident there will be productions, restaurants, and a special group of talented artists to continue this great tradition that will always convey the richness and diversity of the theatrical feast that is New York.

The show will go on.

To those just coming onto the scene, Bon appetit!

Bibliography

Bach, Steven. *Dazzler*, Alfred A. Knopf, New York, 2001

Billington, Michael. *Peggy Ashcroft*, John Murray, 1998

Brown, Dennis. *Actors Talk*, Proscenium Publishers Inc., New York, 1999

Brown, Jared. *The Fabulous Lunts*, Atheneum, New York, 1986

Cook, Peter. *Something Like Fire*, ed. Lin Cook, Methuen, 1996

Coveney, Mike and Stephens, Robert. *Knight Errant*, Hodder & Stoughton, London, 1995

Day, Barry. *This Wooden O*, Oberon, 1996

Frewin, Leslie. *The Late Mrs. Dorothy Parker*, Macmillan, New York, 1986

Gaines, James R. *Wit's End. Days and Nights of the Algonquin Round Table*, 1977 (excerpt reprinted by permission of Harcourt Inc.)

Hall, Peter. *Diaries*, ed. John Goodwin, Hamish Hamilton, London, 1983

Hart, Moss. *Act One*, St. Martin's Press, New York, 1959

Kriendler, H. Peter (with H. Paul Jeffers). *21*, Taylor Publishing, Dallas, Texas, 1999

Lang, George. *Nobody Knows the Truffles I've Seen*, Alfred A. Knopf, New York, 1999

Mead, Marion. *What Fresh Hell Is This?*, Penguin Books, Harmondsworth, 1989

Miller, John. *With a Crack in Her Voice*, Weidenfeld & Nicolson, London, 1998

Morehouse III, Ward. *Inside the Plaza*, Applause Books, New York, 2001

Morley, Sheridan. *John Gielgud*, Simon & Schuster, New York, 2002

Naughton, Anita. *Tea & Sympathy*, G.P. Putnam's Sons, New York, 2002

Rich, Frank. *Ghost Light*, Random House, New York, 2000

Sardi Jr., Vincent and West, Edward. *Off the Wall at Sardi's*, Applause Books, New York, 1995

Sharland, Elizabeth. *From Shakespeare to Coward*, Barbican, 1999

Sher, Antony. *Beside Myself*, Hutchinson/Random House, London, 2001

Tynan, Kenneth. *The Diaries of Kenneth Tynan*, ed. John Lahr, Bloomsbury, London, 2001

Tynan, Kenneth. *Profiles*, ed. K. Tynan and E. Eban, Hern, London, 1999

Villas, James. *Between Bites*, John Wiley & Sons, New York, 2002

Index

Academy of Music 46
Acting Company, the 98
actors
 ad libs 146–7
 apartments, guide to
  193–7
 awards 8, 31, 169, 171,
  172, 192, 195, 197
 charities for 47, 49–50, 198
 portraits/caricatures of
  7–8, 38–41
 pressures of performance
  144–6, 176–8
 retired, care of 49–50
Actors Equity Association
 40, 46
Actors' Fund of America 47,
 50
Actors' Guild, Episcopal
 199–200
Actors Talk (Brown) 174–6
ad libs 146–7
Adams, Charles 80
Adams, Franklin Pierce 38,
 74
afternoon tea 62, 171
Albee, Edward F. 60
Aldwych Theatre (London)
 132, 153
Alessandrini, Gerard 97
Algonquin Hotel
 cuisine 178
 guest-list 24–5
 Oak Room 25, 27, 149
 Rose Room 75
 Round Table 25–7, 74–92,
  127, 149, 152
 origins of 74–5
 wit of 75–6
Algonquin Hotel ix, 2, 24–7,
 108, 118, 119, 148–9,
 177, 178

Alice's Fourth Floor 98
Allen, Gracie 51
Allen, Joe 93
Allen, Woody 19
Allied Relief Ball 128
Allinson, Michael 38
Alvin Theater (later Neil
 Simon Theater) 20
Ames, Beatrice 90
Amherst, Jeffrey 117
Anderson, Brooks 196
Anderson, Maxwell 68
Andrews, Bobby 109
Andrews, Harry 68
Andrews, Julie 4, 97, 127,
 165, 177, 194
Ansonia, The 192–3
Anything Goes (Porter) 32
Aquitania (ocean liner) 117
architecture 37, 50, 56, 59,
 187–8
Armstrong, Louis 18
Arnaz, Lucy 164
Arnold, Tom 109
Arnott, Edward 47
Art Deco 35, 101, 108, 190,
 197
Arthur (film) 28, 149
Ashcroft, Peggy 68–70, 141,
 170
Astaire, Fred 31, 46, 81,
 197
Astor family 17, 59
Astor Hotel 128, 159
Astor Place riots 63
Atkins, Eileen 164, 167–8
Atkinson, Brook 140–1
Averell Harrimans, the 79
Ayckbourn, Alan 173–4

Bacall, Lauren 29
Bach, Steven 128

Bagnold, Edith 67
Baked Alaskas 19
Baker, Jean Claude 169
Baker, Josephine 20
Balestier, John A. 48
Ballantine's Scotch 14–15
Bankhead, Tallulah 24,
 196–7, 199
Barbetta's 93
Barclay, Henry A. 48
Barnes, Clive 161, 166
Barrett, Lawrence 39
Barrie, J.M. 76
Barrymore, Ethel 129
Barrymore family 24, 74
Barrymore, John 38, 39, 154
Barrymore, Lionel 81
Barrymore, Maurice 49
Barrymore Theater 106,
 171, 197
Bart, Lionel 181, 182
Bates, Alan 164, 166, 195
Beard, James 12
Beaumont, Binkie 67, 90
Beckett, Harry 47
Beckett, Samuel 177
Bedroom Farce (Ayckbourn)
 173–4
Behan, Brendan 24, 34, 161
Belasco, David 46, 57
Benchley, Robert 13, 18, 25,
 87
 and Algonquin Round
  Table 74, 75, 78, 79, 82,
  84
Bennett, Alan 94, 97, 166,
 167
Bennett, Arnold 73
Benny, Jack 51
Benny, Mary Livingstone 51
Bentley, Walter Edmund
 198

204

Berle, Milton 53, 58
Berlin, Irving 46, 53, 55, 57, 127, 195
Bernhardt, Sarah 7
Berns, Charlie 12–14
bistros 20
Blakemore, Michael 173
Block, Jesse 51
Bloom, Claire 96
boarding houses 114, 131
Bogart, Humphrey 16
Bolton, Guy 153
Booth, Edwin 6, 37, 39, 41–3, 199
Booth, Junius Brutus 39, 42
Booth Theater 149–50
Booth's Theater 46
Boucicault, Dion 6, 49
Bowery Bar 150–1
Boyer, Lucienne 18
Brando, Marlon 144–5
Brandreth, Gyles 150–1
Brendan Behan's New York (Behan) 34
Brice, Fanny 81
Brideshead Revisited (TV drama) 167, 168
Brigadoon (Lerner and Loewe) 25, 111
British theater 136–7, 159, 166, 173–4, 181
   classical 136, 137, 147, 160, 178
   drama critics 167–8
   stars of, on Broadway 62–70, 164–85, 197
Broadhurst theater 81
Broadway
   and British theater 136–7, 159, 166, 173–4, 181
   in early days 6–7, 46
   and off-Broadway 93–4, 99
   opening/closing nights 26, 36, 70
   stars of 127–42
   British 62–70, 164–85, 197
   walks around 186–97
Broadway ix–x 47, 105–8, 110, 118–19
Brooks Anderson Theater 196–7
Brooks, Louise 157
Brooks, Mel 157
Broun, Heywood 75, 82

Brown, David 16
Brown, Jared 133
Brown, Tina 23, 157
Browne's Chop House 52
Bryant's 46
Brynner, Yul 4, 52, 60
   interest in food 134–5
Buchanan, Jack 70, 115
Burke, Billie 106
Burnett, Carol 51
Burns, George 51
Burton, Richard 127, 137–9, 141, 177, 194
Burton, Sybil 177

cabaret 124–5
Café Cino 99
Café des Artistes 9–11
   murals in 10, 11
Café La Ma Ma 99
Café Un, Deux, Trois 185
Cagney, James 38, 41
Caine, Michael 19
Caldwell, Zoë 167, 168
Camelot 137–8, 194
Campbell, Alan 86–7, 88, 90, 91–2
Campbell, Mrs. Patrick 28, 30, 67–8, 69, 188
Campbell, Naomi 23
Cantor, Eddie 60
Cap d'Antibes 84–5
Capote, Truman 29
Caravelle, La 16–17
Careless Rapture (Novello) 107–8
caricatures 7–8
Carmen's Restaurant 194
Carnegie, Andrew 59
Carnegie Deli 150
Caruso, Enrico 28, 57, 193
Cats (Lloyd Webber) 183
Central Park 2, 191
Channing, Carol 4, 134
Chaplin, Charlie 24, 33, 85
Charles, Richard L. 47
Charlot, André 115
Chatterton, Ruth 123
chefs 12
Chelsea Girls, The (film) 34
Chelsea Hotel 140
Cherry Lane Theater 96–7
Chesterton, G.K. 73
Chevalier, Maurice 81

Chez Josephine 20, 169
Christy, Howard Chandler 10
Church of the Trans-figuration 198–9
churches 198–201
Churchill, Winston 190
Churchill's 6
Cino, Joe 99
Circle in the Square 94
Claiborne, Craig 19
Claire, Ina 25, 111
Clarke, Arthur C. 34
classical theater 136, 137, 147, 160, 178
Clemens, Samuel L. *see* Mark Twain
Clinical Research Bureau 35
Clinton, Bill 12
Close Harmony (Parker/Rice) 80–1
Clubhouse, the 51, 55
clubs 36–61
   women in 51–2
   see also individual clubs
Coburn, Charles 38
Cocktail Party, The (Eliot) 146
cocktails 19, 111
Codron, Michael 182
Cohan, George M. 7, 28, 46, 194
   and Friars Club 53, 55, 56–7
   memorials of 54, 189, 196
Collier, Willie 55
Collins, Pauline 168–9
Collins, Seward 83, 84
Colman, Ronald 112
Colony, the 16, 111, 122
Connelly, Marc 75, 80, 81
Conti, Tom 164, 166
Cook, Charles Emerson 55
Cook, Ralph 99
Cooke, Alistair 143–4
Cooper Diner 151
Cooper, Gladys 67
Cooper, Wyatt 92
Corbett, Gentleman Jim 53
Cornell, Katharine 128, 197
Cote Basque 122
Cotton Club, the 32
Courtenay, Tom 94, 166–7, 197

Courtneidge, Cicely 109
Courtney, Marguerite 112
Coveney, Michael 164
Covent Garden
  actors' church 200
  Theater Museum 119,
  182
Coward, Noël 1–2, 3, 9, 31,
  67, 81, 111–26, 127, 135,
  137, 142, 149
  on Broadway 114, 118–19,
  120, 123–4, 158
  in cabaret 124
  early visits to New York
  111–14
  favorite dishes 1, 173
  favorite hotels 24, 75, 87
  favourite restaurants 111,
  122–3
  and Ivor Novello 100, 104
  love for America 113, 116,
  126
  money problems 111, 114,
  119, 120, 124, 125
  patriotism of 118, 122
  in Second World War
  122–3
  social life 111–12, 113,
  128, 190
  on television 125
  dies 126
Cox, Brian 146, 164
Crawford, Michael 172
Crisp, Quentin 149, 150–1
Cronkite, Walter 46
Crosby, Bing 60, 87, 200
Crowninshield, Frank 13,
  72–3, 74, 75, 77
cuisine
  American 20–1, 22
  British 22
  fast food 194
  French 16
  modern 19
  see also dishes
Cumming, Alan 164, 185
customers, vetting 12
Cyrano 8

Dale, Jim 94, 172, 181, 194
Dana, Charles A. 49
dancing 17, 27–8
  revolving dance floors 18,
  101

Dancing Years, The
  (Novello) 107
Dankworth, John 148
Davidson, Gordon 25
Day, Barry 147
De Mille, Cecil B. 46
Delacorte Theater 191–2
Delacourt, George Jr 192
Delf, Harry 58, 60
Delmonico's 6, 47, 66
Dempsey, Jack 53
Dench, Judi 4, 169–72, 192
  receives Gielgud Award
  169–70
Design for Living (Coward)
  114, 185
Devlin, Mary 42
Dewey, Thomas E. 46
Dexter, John 173, 174–6
Dickens, Charles 3
  reading tours 63–6
Dietrich, Marlene 101, 124,
  165
Diller, Phyllis 51
Dillon, Tom 47
Disenchanted, The ix–x
dishes 133
  actors' favorites 1, 17,
  172–3
  see also cuisine
Distel, Sacha 29
Dixon, Adele 70
Dockstader, Lew 55
Domingo, Placido 95
Don't Tell Mama 196
Douglas Fairbanks Theater
  98
Douglas, Michael 16, 30
Downey's ix, 162
Dr. Round's (boarding
  house) 114, 131
drama critics 4, 8–9, 25–6,
  76–7, 115–16, 140–1,
  152–63, 166
  awards 167
  influence of 160–3
  US and British, differences
  between 167–8
Dreiser, Theodore 7
Drew, John 25, 74
Dreyfuss, Richard 25
Drury Lane 108, 180
du Maurier, Gerald 140
Duchamp, Marcel 11

Duchin, Peter 18
Duffy (cartoonist) 75
Dufy, Raoul 16, 73
dumb waiters 11
Duncan, Isadora 9, 11, 85
Durante, Jimmy 41, 60
Dylan, Bob 34

Eastwood, Clint 19
Edison Hotel 35
Edward VIII (ex-king) 2, 31,
  102, 116–17
Ehle, Jennifer 185
Eighth Avenue ix
Eisenhower, Dwight D. 47
Elaine's 19
Eliot, T.S. 73, 146, 183
Elizabeth II, Queen 12
Ellington, Duke 18
Eloise 29, 30
Eloise at the Plaza
  (Thompson/Knight) 29
Eltinge, Julian 55
Englewood, NJ 50
Enough Rope (Parker) 83
entertainment 17, 18, 101,
  124–5
Enthoven, Gabrielle 119
Episcopal Actors' Guild
  199–200
Equus (Shaffer) 139, 174–6
Erdmann, Martin 59
Erlanger Theater 194
Ethel Barrymore Theater
  106, 171, 197
Evans, Harold 23
Evans, Maurice 69
Evans, Ross 91
Everett, Rupert 23
Everglades, The 6
Eyre, Lawrence 81
Eyre, Richard 170, 172, 173,
  178

Fairbanks, Douglas 24–5, 46,
  57, 60, 74, 81, 148, 200
  Theater 98
Fairbanks, Douglas Sr. 41,
  154
Fall (Christy) 10
Farrow, Mia 29
fast food 194
Ferber, Edna 9, 13, 25, 129
Ferrer, José 8, 41

Fields, W.C. 46, 60
Finney, Albert 164–5, 166–7, 194, 197
Fiorello's 95
first nights *see* opening/ closing nights
First World War 49, 100, 103, 115, 119, 155
Fitzgerald, F. Scott 13, 27, 78, 84, 87, 186, 189
Fitzgerald, Geraldine 96
Fitzgerald, Zelda 27–8, 78, 84, 189
Flagg, James Montgomery 40
Fontanne, Lynne 4, 75, 114, 130–4
  relationship with Alfred Lunt 130–1, 132
food
  provided by diners 10–11
  serving customs x
  see also cuisine; dishes
"Food for Thought" (readings) 99
Forbidden Broadway (show) 97
Ford Theater (Washington D.C.) 55–6
Forrest, Edwin 38, 63
Fountain Girl (Christy) 10
Four Seasons 11–12
Foy, Eddie 46
Frankie and Johnnie's 159
Friars Club 3, 36, 51–61
  Abbots 53, 54, 55, 56–7, 58
  anthem 55
  charity work 53–4
  Clubhouses 51, 55, 56, 58
  "Martin Erdmann Resi-dence" 59–60
  "Friars Frolics" 55, 56, 57
  membership 51–2, 56, 57
  origins 52, 54–5
  Testimonial/Celebrity Dinners 55, 56, 61
  women in 51–2, 57
Friars Foundation 53–4
Friars Monastery 51
Frohman, Charles 7
Frohman, Daniel 195
Fronton, the 12–13
fundraising 147–9

Gaiety Restaurant 44

Gaines, James R. 26–7
Gallagher, Helen 20–1
Gallagher's Steak House 20–1, 152
Garden of Allah (Hollywood hotel) 87
Gardner, Ava 190
Garland, Judy 127
Gay's the Word (Novello) 109
Gershwin, George 20, 81, 127, 129
Gershwin, Ira 20, 127
Gielgud, Sir John 3, 24, 36, 41, 43, 68, 70, 137, 140, 141, 170
  Award 169–70
  obituary 28
Gilbert and Sullivan 66–7
Gilbert, Olive 109
Gilbert, W.S. 66, 155
Gish, Lillian 25, 68
Gladstone Hotel 120
Glaenzer, George 81
Glamorous Night (Novello) 107, 108
Glass Menagerie (Williams) 142
Globe Theater 147–8
Guild 147
Goddard, Paula 85
Goodman, Marshall 38
Gordon, Ruth 25, 68, 84
Gormé, Edie 51
Gottlieb, Morton 141
Governor's Island 147
Grace, Princess *see* Kelly, Grace
Gramercy Park 36, 37, 99
Grateful Dead, The 34
Gray, Simon 166
Great Depression 17–18, 20, 58
Greenwich Village 12
Gregory, Lady 24, 75
Griffith, D.W. 104
Grimes, Tammy 185
Grizzard, George ix–x
Guinness, Alec 30, 123, 135, 146–7
Guthrie's 123

Habeas Corpus (Bennett) 166

Hall, Sir Peter 4, 24, 170, 172, 173–4
Hamlet 137
Hammerstein, Oscar II 46, 57, 60
Hammett, Dashiell 88
Hampden, Walter 41
Hampden-Booth Theater library 36, 40–1
Hampton, Christopher 160
Hard Rock Café 150
Hare, David 4, 24, 160, 167, 169, 178
Hare, John 45
Harlem 32
Harold Clurman Theater 98
Harrigan's Theater 46
Harris, Julia 96, 131
Harris, Richard 138
Harris, Rosemary 148, 167, 185
Harrison, Rex 94, 138, 141, 146, 177, 197, 198, 199
Hart, Bernie ix
Hart, Kitty Carlisle, ix, 127
Hart, Moss ix, 4, 33, 138–9
  career 127–8
  favorite restaurants 128
  and George Kaufman 127, 128–30
Hart's Theater 46
Harwood, Ronald 167
Havoc, June 166
Hawks, Wells 55
Hawthorne, Nigel 197
Hawtrey, Charles 140
Hay Fever (Coward) 1–2, 112
Hayes, Helen 69, 87, 129, 133, 142
  Theater 193
Hayward, Leland 87
Hearst, William Randolph 88
Hecht, Ben 87
Heifetz, Jascha 81
Hellman, Lillian 88, 90
Hemingway, Ernest 82, 84, 85, 89
Hendrix, Jimi 34
Henry Miller Theater 81
Hepburn, Katharine 40, 85, 131

Herbert, Victor 7, 46, 55
Hershfield, Harry 58, 60
Hicks, Seymour 153
Hiller, Wendy 68
Hilton, Conrad 28
Hirschfeld, Al 38
Hitchcock, Alfred 105
Holbrook, Hal 170
Holland, Edmund M. 48
Hollywood 33, 82, 86, 87, 90, 91, 134–5, 137, 165
Hollywood Anti-Nazi League 88
Holm, Celeste 25, 166
Hope, Bob 123, 143, 200
Hopkins, Anthony 24
Hopper, De Wolf 55
Horowitz, Vladimir 17
Hostage, The (Behan) 161–2
Hotel Bristol (Paris) 16
Hotel Chelsea 33–5
Hotel des Artistes 10–11
Hotel Edison 58, 197
Hotel Hermitage 54–5
hotels 24–35
    see also individual hotels
Houghton, George Hendric 199
Howard, Leslie 68, 129, 196
Howe, Buddy 60
Humphries, Barry 149
Hunnicut, Arthur 25
Hunter, Kim 97, 142, 144
Hurst, Fannie 11, 84
Huston, Angelica 51
Huston, Walter 25
Huxley, Aldous 87

ice machines 11
Illington, Margaret 195
INTAR Hispanic American Arts Center 98
Irons, Jeremy 3, 24
Irving, Henry 7, 36, 49, 63
Isherwood, Christopher 87

J. Lester Wallack's Theater 46
Jackson, Glenda 178
Jacobi, Derek 178
Jacobs, Harry Alan 56
Jagger, Mick 30
Jamaica 108, 125–6

Jammet, André 16–17
jazz 81
Jekyll and Hyde 150
Jefferson, Joseph 39
Jessel, George 60
Joe Allen's 93, 196
John Houseman Center 98
John Paul II, Pope 12
Jolson, Al 46, 60
Joplin, Janis 34
journalists 13

Kaufman, George F. 4, 13, 25, 26, 80, 81, 90
    and Moss Hart 127, 128–30
    Theater 98
Kazan, Elia 144–5
Keach, Stacey 96
Kean, Edmund 62, 63
Keane, Doris 69
Keene's Chop House 49, 52
Kelly, Father 200–1
Kelly, Gene 31
Kelly, Grace (later princess) 12, 16, 19, 147, 190
Kelly, Jude 160
Kemble, Charles 62
Kemble, Fanny 6, 62
Kendall, Mr/Mrs 62
Kennedy family 16
Kennedy, Jackie 16, 19
Kennedy, John F. 27
Kern, Jerome 154–5
Kerr, Walter 162
King Cole Room (St. Regis Hotel) 152
King and I, The 134, 135
King's Rhapsody (Novello) 107, 108–9
Kirkland, Muriel 40
kitchens 30
    pullman 10–11
Kitt, Eartha 29
Kline, Kevin 25, 95, 96
Knight, Hilary 29
Koch, Mayor Edward I. 54
Kovacs, Ernie 8
Kriendler, Jack 12–14

La Guardia, Mayor Fiorello 11
Lahr, Bert 46
Lahr, John 157

Laine, Cleo 148
Lamb, Charles 44–5
Lamb, Mary 44–5
Lambs Club 3, 36, 44–50
    aims/ideals of 48
    Council of 48
    origin of 47
    roster of members 46–7, 49
    traditions in 50
    venues for 48–9, 50, 195
Lang, George 11–12
Langan's 21–2
Langella, Frank 160
Langtry, Lillie 3, 7, 63
Lansbury, Angela 4, 24, 195
Lapotaire, Jane 172
Las Vegas 124
Lauder, Harry 63
Laughton, Charles 24
Laurencin, Marie 73
Lawrence, D.H. 73
Lawrence, Gertrude ix, 24, 81, 115, 128, 194
Laye, Evelyn 70
Leigh, Vivien 9, 29, 136, 137
Lerner, Alan J. 25, 46
Levine, James 11
Lewis, Joe E. 53, 58
Lewis, Sinclair 87
Lewis, Ted 60
Lewis, William 87
libraries
    Hampden-Booth Theater 36, 40–1
    Players Club 36, 40–1
Library of the Performing Arts 8
Life (magazine) 78
Lillie, Beatrice (Bea) 18, 24, 40, 101, 106
Lincoln Center 8, 9, 95
Lindbergh, Charles 46
Lindsay, Robert 172
Lindy's building 58
liquor
    brands 14–15
    with meals 155–6
Lithgow, John 168
Little Church 198–9
Lloyd, Marie 63
Lloyd Webber, Andrew 4, 97, 101, 183
Loewe, Frederick 25, 46
Lombard, Carole 87

INDEX

London 90–1, 93, 100,
108–9, 167
wartime 132
London Lambs 44
Long Island 49–50
Lonsdale, Frederic 197
Look after Lulu (Coward)
158
Lotos Club 50
Louys, Pierre 76–7
Luchow's 6, 122
Lucille Lortel Theater 96
Luhan, Mabel Dodge 83–4
Lumley, Joanna 23
Lunt, Alfred 4, 25, 33, 75,
90, 114, 129, 130–4
cookery of 131, 132, 133–4
relationship with Lynn
Fontanne 130–1
Lunts, the 131–4, 186
Lunts, The Fabulous
(Brown) 133
Lyceum Theater 195

McArthur, Charles 78–9
McCormack, John 81
McEwan, Geraldine 170, 178
McIndoe, Angus 185
McKellen, Ian 24, 147, 172
Mackintosh, Cameron 4,
179–84
early life 179–80
wealth 180, 182
McLean, George 47
MacLeish, Archibald/Ada
84
McMein, Neysa 77, 186
McNally, Terence 99
McPherson, Aimee Semple
83
Macready, William 62, 63
"Mad Dogs and English-
men" (Coward) 123
Madonna 21, 97
Maeterlinck, Maurice 11
Maison Doree Hotel 48
Majestic Theater 194
Malden, Karl 144
Manhattan 12, 98, 101, 117
Manhattan Plaza 98–9
Manhattan Theater Club
(MTC) 94
Mann, Theodore 94
Manners, Hartley 142

Mansfield, Richard 68
Marriott Hotel 190–1
Marsh, Jean 165–6, 167
Martin Beck Theater 140,
195–6
"Martin Erdmann
Residence" 59–60
Martin, Mary 123–4
Martin, Millicent 148
Marx, Harpo 75, 85, 129
Mason, Jackie 21, 150
"Matchbox, The" 48–9
Matinée Idles 164
matinées ix–x 141, 146, 171
Matisse, Henri 73
Matthews, Charles 62
Matthews, Jessie 177–8
Maugham, Somerset 24, 67,
84, 87, 190
Maxim's 6
Maxwell, Elsa 32, 85, 106–7
May, Elaine 173
Meadow, Lynne 94
Mencken, H.L. 13
Menken, Helen 25
Mercanton, Louis 104
Meredith, Burgess 25
Metropolitan Opera 173,
174
MGM 87
Millay, Edna St. Vincent 12
Miller, Arthur 34
Miller, Henry 7
Miller, John 169, 171
Miller, Jonathan 24
Miller, Marilyn 26
Milne, A.A. 85
Minetta Lane Theater 97
Minnelli, Liza 25, 30, 51
mint juleps 111
Miserables, Les 109, 183–4
Mitzi E. Newhouse Theater
95
Monroe, Marilyn 190
Montague, Henry J. 44, 47
Moore, Dan 37
Moore, Dudley 28, 149
Moore, Roger 148–9
Morgan, Frank 38
Morley, Robert 140–1, 142
Morosco Theater 81
Mosher, Robert 98
Mountbatten, Lady Edwina
81

Mountbatten, Lord Louis 81,
123
Mousetrap, The (Christie)
184
Muir, Jean 19
murals 10, 11, 16
Murphy, Gerald/Sara 84, 86,
89
Murray, Bill 75
Murrow, Edward R. 60
Music Box Theater 195
music-hall 63
My Fair Lady (Lerner and
Loewe) 25, 146, 165

Nabokov, Vladimir 34
Nast, Condé 77
Nast, Thomas 38
Nathan, George Jean 25
National Theatre 17, 136,
137, 167, 171, 174
Naughton, Anita 22, 23
Neeson, Liam 164, 178
Neil Simon Theater 20
Neshobe Island 78, 82
New Amsterdam Theater
55
New York
19th Century 45
walks in 186–97
New York Friars *see* Friars
Club
New York Shakespeare
Festival 95
New York Times 8–9, 25,
152, 159
influence of 160–1
New York World 12
New Yorker 8, 80, 85–6, 87,
89, 92, 152, 156–7
Newman, Paul 11
Nicholas Nickleby (RSC) 196
Nichols, Mike 173
Night and Day (film) 33
Niven, David 15, 125
*Nobody Knows the Truffles
I've Seen* (Lang) 11–12
North, Oliver 21
Novello Davies, Clara 102–3,
106
Novello, Ivor 3, 31, 100–10,
122, 190
early life 102–3
on Broadway 105–6, 107–8

favorite hotels/restaurants
  108
film career 103–5
and Noël Coward 100, 104
in West End 108–9
Nunn, Trevor 24, 171

Oak Room (Plaza Hotel) 25,
  27, 128, 189
Obie Awards 94, 96
ocean liners 108, 111, 117,
  121, 147
O'Connor, Carroll 25
off-Broadway 93–9
  awards 94, 96
  types of production/venue
    93–4, 98
Oh Calcutta! 156–7
O'Hara, John 13
Old Vic Company 136, 137,
  139, 157
Oliver! (Bart) 181, 182
Olivier, Lawrence 9, 24, 36,
  43, 90, 135–7, 141, 194,
  197
Once in a Lifetime (Hart)
  130
O'Neill, Eugene 46, 68, 94
opening/closing nights 26,
  36, 70, 107, 161–2
opera 46, 66–7, 101–2
Opera House 95
Orso's 93
Osborne, John 156, 166, 195
Oscars 8, 171
"Over There" (Cohan) 57

Pabst's 6
Pagis, Jean 16
Palace Theatre (London)
  108–9
Paley, William 33
Palm Court (Plaza Hotel)
  62
Papp, Joseph 95, 192
Paris 85, 88, 93, 132
Parker, Dorothy 2, 13, 33,
  111, 186
  early life 71–4
  affairs/marriages 73–4,
    78–9, 85, 86–8, 90–1
  and Algonquin Round
    Table 25, 27, 71–92, 152
  depression 79, 82

drinking habit 79, 81–2,
    85–6, 91
  in Europe 84–5, 88
  in Hollywood 86, 87, 90
  and New Yorker 80, 83,
    85–6, 92
  political activities 88–90,
    91
  and Vanity Fair 72–3, 74,
    76–8, 154
  writings 80–1, 82–4, 86,
    87, 90
  reviews 76–7, 83–4, 85–6
  dies 92
Parker, Edwin Pond 73–4
Parrot Girl (Christy) 10
Pastor, Tony 46
Pavarotti, Luciano 12
Pavillon, Le 16, 122
Peacock Alley (Waldorf
  Astoria) 31, 100
Perlman, Itzhak 11
Peters, Bernadette 25
Phillips, Sian 95
Pickford, Mary 57
Pinter, Harold 140, 195
Pirates of Penzance (Gilbert
  and Sullivan) 66–7
Planet Hollywood 150
Players Club 3, 36–43
  architecture of 37, 38, 39
  artifacts at 38, 41, 42
  artworks in 38–41, 42
  Booth Room 41–3
  Card Room 41
  Dining Room 40
  Great Hall 39
  Grill Room 38
  library 36, 40–1
  "roast" tradition 36
Playwright Horizons 98
playwrights 25–6, 67–8,
  93–4, 99
Plaza Hotel 2, 27–30, 128,
  187
  courting tradition 188
  films/writing featuring
    28–30
  Grand Ballroom 29
  Oak Room 25, 27, 128, 189
  Oyster Bar 29, 189
  Palm Court 62, 187–9
  Persian Room 29
Plimpton, George 19

Plowright, Joan 137, 174,
  195
Plummer, Amanda 184–5
Plummer, Christopher
  169–70, 184
Plymouth Theater 196
Poe, Edgar Allan 74
Ponce de Leon (Christy) 10
Porter, Cole 3–4, 85, 127,
  190, 197
  lifestyle 31–3
Porter, Gen. Horace 49
Porter, Linda 32, 33
Press Agents' Association 52
Priestley, J.B. 67
Private Lives (Coward) 121,
  139
Prohibition 12–14, 107, 156
  end of 14–15, 20
Provence, France 84–5
Pryce, Jonathan 181
pullman kitchens 10–11
Puncheon Club 12–14, 80

Q.E.2 147
Quant, Mary 19
Queen Mary ix

Rainbow Room 17–19,
  100–1, 190
  cuisine 18–19
  dance floor 101
Rainbow in the Stars (night-
  club) 17
Rainier, Prince 190
Randell, Louis P. 58
Randolph, Joyce 47
Rattigan, Terence 67
Raye, Martha 51
Rector's 6–7, 62
  described 6
Redgrave, Corin 4, 24, 164
Redgrave family 164, 185
Redgrave, Lynn 4, 24, 37,
  97, 164, 193, 197
Redgrave, Michael 197
Redgrave, Vanessa 4, 21, 24,
  164, 168, 170, 192
Restaurant Row 93–5, 196
restaurants 6–23, 150–1,
  186–97
  see also individual
    restaurants
restoration 18, 101

reviews *see* drama critics
Reza, Yasmina 4
Rice, Elmer 80
Rich, Frank 4, 152, 159–63
Richardson, Natasha 3, 25, 97
Richardson, Ralph 135, 137, 140, 157
Rigg, Diana 24, 172
Ringling, John 57
Ritz, the 24
Rivers, Joan 51–2
Robards, Jason 25, 96
Roberts, Rachel 139, 166
Robertson, Forbes 62
Robeson, Paul 75, 104
Rockefeller Plaza *see* Rainbow Room
Rockefeller family 17–18
Rockwell, Norman 38
Rodgers, Richard 75
Rogers, Ginger 31
Rogers, Will 46, 55, 60
Romberg, Sigmund 46
Roosevelt, Eleanor 8
Rose, Richard 106
Ross, Harold 74–5, 80, 83, 89
Round, Dr. 114, 131
Round Table 25–7
Royal Shakespeare Company 136, 178, 196
Royalton Hotel 82
Russell, Rosalind 40, 200

St. James's Theater 194
St. Malachy's 200–1
St. Regis Hotel 136, 189–90
King Cole Room 152
Samuel Beckett Theater 98
Samuels, Art 75
Sanger, Margaret 35
Sardi, Vincent Jr. 8, 9
Sardi's ix, x, 2, 6, 7–9, 108, 150, 155, 162, 163
Sardi's, Off the Wall at (Sardi) 8
Sargent, John Singer 39
Savoy Hotel (London) 104, 132
Savoy, the 24
Schrader, Frederick F. 54
Scofield, Paul 178
Scott, George C. 96

Screen Writers' Guild 88
Second World War 11, 90, 122–3, 132
Secret Rapture (Hare) 160
Segal, George 139
Selznick, David O. 136
Shaffer, Peter 139, 176
Shakespeare Guild 169
Shakespeare productions 136, 137, 147, 160
open-air 191–2
Shakespeare Theater Workshop 95
Shakespeare's Garden (Central Park) 191
Shanley's Moulin Rouge 6
Shaw, Fiona 99
Shaw, George Bernard 67–8, 81, 84
Sheldon, Edward 68, 69
Shepard, Sam 99
Sher, Antony 30–1
Sherrin, Ned 179
Sherwood, Robert E. 25, 33, 74, 78, 87, 133
Shields, Brooke 51
Shore, Dinah 51
Short, Bobby 19
Shubert, Lee 57, 60
Shubert Organization 193–4, 195
Shubert Theater 193–4
Shuberts, the 106
Side by Side (Sondheim) 181
Sidgwick, Edie 34
Simon, Neil 30
Simpson, Wallis 2, 31
Sinatra, Barbara 51
Sinatra, Frank 29, 52, 53
Sinden, Donald 166
Smith, Alfred E. 57
Smith, Jo 60
Smith, Liz 21
Smith, Maggie 4, 30, 164, 197
Solomon, Jack 20–1
Sondheim, Steven 29, 181
Soule, Henri 16
Sousa, John Philip 46
Southern, E.H. 49
Spain 85, 89
Spanish Civil War 89
speakeasies 12–14, 16, 20

Spelvin, George 26
Spring (Christy) 10
Stage Door Canteen 132
Stanford White building 195
steak houses 20–1, 122, 152
Stein, Gertrude 73
Stephens, Robert 164–5
Stern, Isaac 11
Stewart, Donald Ogden 82, 87–8
Stewart, Ellen 99
Stickney, Dorothy 25
Stoppard, Tom 24
Stork Club 111
Stow, John A. 48
Strasberg, Susan 141
Streep, Meryl 96
Streetcar Named Desire, A (Williams) 144–6
Streisand, Barbra 51
Stritch, Elaine 19
Suchet, David 172–3
Sullivan, Arthur 66–7
Sullivan, Ed 53, 60
Sully, Eva 51
Sully, Robert 39
Sunshine Committee 53
Supper Club 171
Swing Girl, The (Christy) 10
Swope, Herbert 12, 82, 86

tables
food prepared at ix, x
producers' ix
Tandy, Jessica 143–6
Taubman, Howard 162
"Tavern on the Green" 192
Taylor, Deems 75
Taylor, Elizabeth 3, 51, 52, 137, 139, 190
Taylor, Laurette 111–12, 131, 142
tea 62, 171
Tea & Sympathy 22–3
Tea Room (Plaza Hotel) 187–9
television 124, 125, 167, 169
Tempest, Marie 63
Ten Chimneys 131, 133, 134
Terry, Ellen 7, 36, 41
Thackeray, William Makepeace 74
Theater Genesis 99
Theater Guild 68, 99

Theater Row 5, 93–9
 opening of 98
theaters in 98–9
Theatre Arielle 98
Theatre de Lys 96
Theatre Museum, Covent
 Garden 119, 182
This Was a Man (Coward)
 120
This Wooden O (Day) 147–8
Thomas, Dylan 34, 139–40
Thompson, Kay 29, 186, 189
Thorndike, Sybil 135
Thurber, James 75, 86, 89
Tilley, Vesta 63
Times Square 34, 190–1, 194
Todd, Mike 3, 52, 53, 60,
 125
Together with Music (TV
 show) 125
Tomlin, Lily 25
Tony awards 171, 172, 195,
 197
Toohey, John Peter 26–7
Town and Country
 (magazine) 19
Tracy, Spencer 46
Treboux, Robert 19
Tree, Herbert Beerbohm 7,
 63
Truman, Harry 8
Trump, Donald 28, 30
Truth Game, The (Novello)
 106
Tucker, Richard 60
Tucker, Sophie 57
Tune, Tommy 25
Turner, Kathleen 11
Tutin, Dorothy 170
Twain, Mark 34, 38, 41, 74
21 (speakeasy) 12–16, 127,
 128, 155
 patrons described 15–16
Tynan, Kenneth 4, 152,
 156–9

Un-American Activities
 Committee 91

Union Square Hotel 48
Upstairs Downstairs (TV
 show) 166, 167
Ustinov, Peter 24

Valentino, Rudolf 9, 85
 funeral of 200
Vanderbilt family 27
Vanderbilt, Gladys 188
Vanderbilt, Gloria 92
Vanity Fair 72–3, 74, 76–8,
 114, 154
Variety 160, 161
vaudeville 58
Veau D'Or, Le 19, 147
Venice 31, 32
Vickers, Hugo 137
Victor/Victoria 165
Village Voice 96
Villas, James 19
Vivian Beaumont Theater
 95
Voisin, Le 16, 122–3, 128
Volney Hotel 91, 92

waiters x, 150, 159
Waldorf Astoria 2, 12, 24,
 31–3, 190
 Cole Porter's piano at 190
 Peacock Alley 31, 100, 190
Walker, George W. 48
Walker, James L. 12, 57, 60
walks in New York 4, 34–5,
 186–97
Wall Street Crash 13, 86,
 105–6, 120–1
Wallack, Arthur 47
Wallack, J. Lester 46
Wallack, John Henry 38
Wanamaker, Sam 147–8
Wanamaker, Zoë 167
Warhol, Andy 29, 34
Washington Place 12
Wayne, John 47
Webb, Clifton 26
"Wedding Cake" building
 192–3
Welles, Orson 24, 25, 197

Wells, H.G. 73
Wesker, Arnold 156, 166,
 174
West End 67, 108–9, 110,
 159, 180–2
Wheeler, Bert 46
White Barn Theater
 (Connecticut) 96
White Horse Tavern 34,
 140
White, Stanford 37, 39
Whitney, Jock 79
Whitney, William Payne 59
Wilde, Oscar 3, 62
Wilder, Thornton 87
Williams, Emlyn 139
Williams, Percy 49–50
Williams, Tennessee 19,
 142
Williamson, Nicol 148, 157,
 158–9
Wilson, Jack 111
Wilson, Lanford 99
Wilson, Sandy 183
Wilson, Woodrow 55–6
Winchell, Walter 7–8,
 13–14, 60
Windsor, Duke of *see*
 Edward VIII
Winters, Roland 38
Wit's End (Gaines) 26–7
Wodehouse, P.G. 3–4, 152–6
 and Jerome Kern 154–5
 plaque for 198
Woollcott, Alexander 11, 13,
 25–6, 69, 74, 76, 78, 80,
 129
Woolworth, F.W. 59
Wright, Frank Lloyd 28
Wyndham, Charles 62
Wyndhams 30–1

York, Michael 148

Zeta-Jones, Catherine 16,
 30
Ziegfeld, Florenz 77, 106,
 179, 193